The Enchanted World

THE BOOK OF CHRISTMAS

The Enchanted World

THE BOOK OF CHRISTMAS

by Brendan Lehane
and the Editors of Time-Life Books

The Content

Time-Life Books · Alexandria, Virginia

THE ETERNAL MOMENT

The heart of Christmas lies in this scene, played out sixty generations past: Through the land of Judaea ran a road, twisting as it climbed among the fields and vineyards that clung to the hillsides, buttressed by rough stone walls. Higher up, the fields gave way to pasture, shaded only by scattered stands of trees: green-leaved oak, silver olive. A squat, stone tower rose there, brooding over sheep that stood with their heads lowered, so many statues caught in the fierce stare of the sun. A mile beyond the tower, on a lofty plateau, houses clustered—thick-walled, flat-roofed, shining white. Beyond them in the flickering distance loomed the purple mountains of Moab.

A line of travelers straggled up the track. Some of these travelers marched along, swinging staffs to mark the pace. Some rode—not on small donkeys but on big, powerful Muscat asses, coated with the dust of the road. Among the riders was a woman, and she was Mary the Virgin, heavy with child. A man strode beside her; he was Joseph, her husband. They had come from Galilee, a nine-day journey, to register for the tax decreed by the Roman Caesar Augustus, who ruled all Is-

rael through petty kings he supported there. Chief among them was Herod, called the Great, a flatterer of the powerful, a despot to the weak. Mary and Joseph, children of a subject people, had obediently journeyed south to Bethlehem, the city of David, son of Jesse, because Joseph was of the family of David and it was required that each man register at the home of his tribe.

They had come also because of prophecy. Far in the past, the spokesmen of Israel's God had foretold that the Savior and King of the Jews would spring from the stem of Jesse; this child of the House of David would free the tribes of Israel from the tyranny of generations of conquerors and bring a new age to the world. The child would be born in David's city. Isaiah had foretold it, and Micah. Now the day had come: Mary, who conversed with angels, bore in her body the Savior, and her time was near. Thus she rode with Joseph to Bethlehem.

As the late light slanted across the hills and set the west ablaze, the couple climbed the last slope into the town, which waited unaware. On its roofs, men sat cross-legged, talking idly in the twilight. The narrow, crowded streets were clouded with the smoke of cook fires and shadowed with violet. At the doorways of

the houses, children played; behind them in dark rooms, oil lamps flickered, making tiny lights in the dusk.

But no door stood open for Mary and Joseph. There was no room at the inn that clung to the hillside, said the chroniclers. The man and woman settled at last, as benighted travelers often did, in a cave below the inn, one of several where the landlord stabled his cattle and sheltered his sheep from the rains and winds, the hungry wolves and jackals of winter. The place was dry and kept warm by the bodies and breath of the oxen that slept there. In its center, on boards of sycamore, stood a manger, a clay trough where the beasts fed on barley stalks and grasses.

Into the dark cave, then, went Mary and Joseph, away from the oil lamps of the town and the busy folk who crowded it. The Judaean night drew in, its darkness spreading swiftly over hillside and town, enfolding all below in a great cloak fretted with silver stars.

In the fields beyond the town, shepherds lay by the tower of the flocks, gathered together so that they might share the watching and have the solace of company. They were toughened men, wrapped in rough woolen capes against the night chill, armed with clubs and slings for fighting off the night predators that threatened their flocks. The sheep were now ranged around the men, rear legs tied to fat tails to keep them from straying. The campfire glowed, an earthbound star on the dark slope. The high notes of a flute curled toward the sky, where Orion wheeled with his studded sword and the Pleiades solemnly danced.

As the night deepened, the flute music trailed off into silence and the shepherds' desultory chatter faded gradually away. Above the fields, Bethlehem slept. So quiet and still lay the hills and town that a sudden cock crow seemed as shrill as a clarion when it sounded across the pastures. The shepherds stirred and peered around, puzzled. The hour was not dawn, after all, but midnight.

And at the cock's crow, time stood still. The shepherds lay as they were, propped on their elbows, their bearded faces turned toward Bethlehem. Sheep drinking from a stream remained unmoving and unbreathing, their muzzles in the water; the stream itself was frozen in motionless ripples of crystal. An owl hung on outstretched wings two feet above the ground; the tiny, marmot-like creature that was its prey remained poised in midstride below it. The night breeze ceased, but a leaf that had floated on it lay in the air, neither fluttering nor falling. The stillness spread all over the waiting world, said the storytellers, and lasted for a time no one could tell.

But then, near Bethlehem, the stillness was broken by movement in the heavens. The stars themselves seemed to tremble and grow near, and as they approached the earth, they took on shape, until the blackness above the heads of the shepherds was filled with wings of light and shining eyes. And as the light grew and formed itself, majestic harmonies swelled in the air. It was as if the stars were singing, enveloping the earth in a diapason of heaven.

As for the shepherds, caught in the

Carolers sang that even the trees of the orchard bowed down to Mary the Virgin. They bent
their laden branches to her hand that she might have cherries by command.

"And Joseph also went up from Galilee, out of the city of
Nazareth, into Judaea, unto the city of David, which is called Bethlehem . . . to be taxed
with Mary, his espoused wife, being great with child."

"And she brought forth her firstborn son, and wrapped him in swaddling clothes, and laid him in a manger, because there was no room for them in the inn."

midst of the glory, they quaked. Then a voice sang, higher than the rest, a clear, bright voice with no hint in it of human mouth or human tongue:

"Fear not," the angel sang. "For, behold, I bring you good tidings of great joy, which shall be to all people. For unto you is born this day in the city of David, a Savior, which is Christ the Lord. And this shall be a sign unto you: Ye shall find the babe wrapped in swaddling clothes, lying in a manger."

The humble cock's crow and the celestial song marked, it seemed, a fold in the centuries, before which nothing and after which everything was bathed in the light the newborn baby brought into the world, an event of such power and consequence that time stumbled in its smooth course and missed a step.

Yet little enough is known of it. Jesus was born to Mary in Bethlehem, in a cave perhaps, or a stable, or even in that room of a house where Jewish peasants sheltered their cattle. Miraculous tokens informed some shepherds nearby; later a great star blazed out in the heavens as sign and guide to some wise men living in countries far to the east that they should journey in search of a newborn King.

That is the whole of the chronicle. The rest is garlands, added by subsequent ages—by monks, scribes, priests, wits, storytellers and common people—to adorn the source of the faith that was their life's greatest treasure. Nothing from the time portrays Joseph, the shepherds, the inn, the innkeepers. The year itself is in doubt, and the time of year a topic merely for speculation and casuistical wrangles. It

would be some three hundred years before the date of the birth was fixed by the elders of the new religion and Christmas was set at the 25th of December.

The reasons for the choice are not difficult to discover: Even a brief glimpse at the stories told about Mary shows how the event was to become the crowning symbol of a thousand years of ritual and custom.

Mary seemed inseparable from flowers. In her youth, the tales say, she shone with purity and loving-kindness; it was clear that the heavens smiled on her. Therefore, the priests of the temple in Nazareth were given the task of choosing her husband. They summoned eligible men to the temple and ordered that each one lay a bare branch on the altar. One branch burst into flower; it was held by Joseph, son of the House of David, and it determined his selection as Mary's husband.

The chroniclers wrote that Joseph was bewildered to find his betrothed with child and that an angel appeared in a dream to tell him Mary bore the Son of God. But the common folk told a different tale. Joseph and Mary walked in a garden, they sang. Mary, astir with the yearnings that all pregnant women feel, asked that he pluck her cherries to eat. Angered, filled with suspicion and reproach, he refused. Let the father of the baby gather cherries, Joseph said. And at once, a voice sang a command in the air. A cherry tree bent its branches so that the fruit fell into her hand. Mary was the rose of the world, said the people; and the child was the very sun of righteousness.

So mother and son brought light to the

"There were in the same country shepherds abiding in the fie[ld]
the Lord came upon them, the glory of the Lord sho[ne]

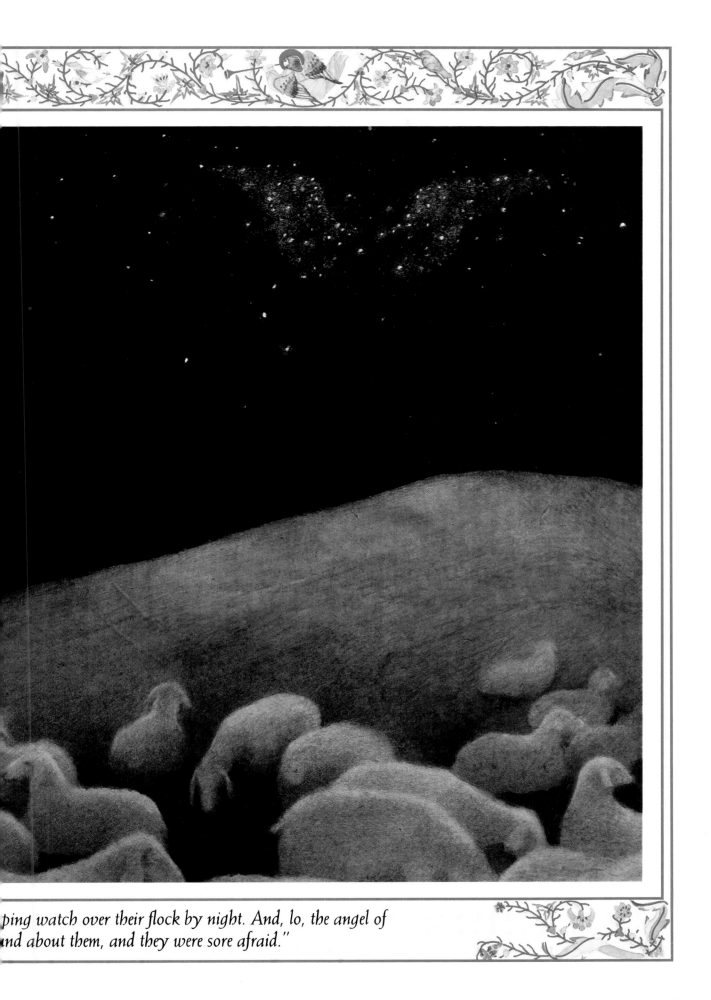

...ping watch over their flock by night. And, lo, the angel of
...nd about them, and they were sore afraid."

darkness and the hope of life to replace the fear of death. Yet the pattern for them, as well as for the rest of the world, was already set: For every people, there lived a ritual that offered hope for despair and the prospect of life in place of death. Those rituals were seasonal; they marked the period of the winter solstice.

The word "solstice" means only "sun stands still." The winter solstice is the point in the yearly course of the earth around the sun when, because of the angle of the earth's axis, the Northern Hemisphere is tilted farthest away from the sun's face. The path that the sun takes across the sky as it travels from horizon to horizon is low. What weak rays reach the earth during that season fall obliquely, offering little light and little warmth. The day of the winter solstice is the shortest of the entire year, and the night the cruelest and the longest.

Most people knew the sun as a god, the provider of light and warmth and life. In late December, the god offered only a brief daily showing, the forced smile of an invalid ancient on his deathbed. Yet in the days that followed, the god fought back against the encroaching darkness, slowly winning through to the midsummer months, when the sun's golden brightness blazed high in the heavens.

People did not take the sun's victory for granted. Men and women then felt themselves and their actions intrinsic to the universe: They had a role to play. They believed that sun and light were truly endangered at the solstice. The earth trembled under the footsteps of the dead, and

unless the living offered prayers and performed ceremonies, death would triumph: There would be no return of summer, no blossoming again of fruits and flowers, no rippling of grain in the fields, no gamboling of infant animals in the pastures.

Far from Bethlehem, far from the ordered rule of the Roman Empire, in the night-black, icy north—the lands of Celt, Geat, Lapp, Finn, Dane and Hun—rituals to ensure the rebirth of the sun were faithfully enacted in massive timbered halls and around fires blazing amid the endless tracts of snow. People masked with horses' heads, with stags' antlers, with deerskins, with the hides of goats, danced in the firelight. They adorned their houses and themselves with holly and ivy and mistletoe and evergreen— all of the plants that withstood the death of winter and so were charged with enchanting power. They held heroic carousals. They sacrificed to the dead and to the gods of darkness: For the sake of the sun and the earth's fertility, animals died, and sometimes men and women.

The threat was not merely the loss of life-giving light, although that was bad enough. The dark, these peoples were certain, was crowded with the creatures of evil. Ghosts haunted the gloom; werewolves prowled; witches, demons, goblins and imps lurked in the nocturn, creating mischief; packs of supernatural dogs massed on the moorlands; malevolent spirits hovered near houses, seeking entrance. So men and women devised ways of cheating them. They chanted protective spells, posted magic symbols on

doors and clothes. And they avoided the dark by making fire.

Fire was at the center of all the winter festivals. It was the brother of the sun, calling out to the heavens. Great bonfires blazed on the hills of Ireland and Scotland, on the mountains of France and Germany and in the halls of the Norse kings. Throughout the countries lapped by the Mediterranean and ruled by Rome, fire burned in the form of candles as the Romans held their winter feast. Originally this feast was called Brumalia; later it became known as the Saturnalia. The festivities were dedicated to the Titan Saturn, lord of the harvest, long trapped by his son Jupiter beneath the earth; perhaps because the imprisoned Titans were deemed to view the world upside down, the Saturnalia was a feast of reversals: Masters served slaves and slaves commanded masters. This was a time of banqueting, of carrying green boughs that signified the strength of life, of bestowing presents. Men and women faced the darkness with a kind of madcap glee, fending it off with their high spirits.

The dates and natures of winter ceremonies and celebrations varied from race to race. Among some peoples, early November was the time for the most concentrated rituals. This was so with the Celts, whose winter began at Samain, November 1. Norsemen originally celebrated Yule — their winter rite — in November, when darkness began to enfold their land. Other festivals were spread throughout the following two months. The Roman Saturnalia occupied the week that ended on the 24th of December. The followers of the Persian god Mithra — the cave-born god of light who drove away the dark — deemed that his birthday was December 25. And many other days in December were the occasions for winter ceremonies. Yet all of them were intimately concerned with the great natural crisis that reached its acme on the day of the sun's shortest and feeblest appearance.

All of these rites were gathered at last under the mantle of the Christian celebration, and while the origins were forgotten, traces of the old ceremonies remained. These traces were to be found in the devotion to the flames of candles and to the blazing of Yule logs, in mimes and mumming and curious rituals and games that echoed ancient and forgotten sacrifices, in feasting and the choice of foods to feast upon, in garlands of holly and ivy and evergreen, in the raising of Christmas trees, in the giving of presents, in the very words of the songs that were sung. The child who was the Son of God and called the sun of righteousness promised delivery from darkness and the hope of everlasting life. The placing of his nativity at the heart of winter seemed natural; it made the new belief a link with the old, and helped keep humankind wedded to the seasons. The attributes of Christmas are those of light and of dark: It is the time for joy and worship, celebration and good will. But these are still spiced with a pleasurable tingle of fear, the relic of an ancient apprehension that flowered on the solstice night, when death and darkness stalked the world.

Days of Winter Magic

Years ago, when life depended on the proper rounds of tilling, sowing, harvesting and the recovery of the sun to begin each cycle anew, not only Christmas but all the days of the winter season were filled with magic. The days were therefore devoted to rituals of the field to ensure good herds and harvests, of the hearth to protect the house, and of the fire to drive away the dark.

In France and Germany and parts of Britain, for instance, winter began on Martinmas – Saint Martin's Day, November 11 – when those gifted with vision might see the saint himself, riding across meadow and field on his white horse, releasing from the folds of his cloak the first snow of the season.

Martin was an early Christian saint, so generous that he cut his cloak in half to warm a freezing beggar and passed the wine cup an emperor gave him to the humblest of his priests. He was the patron of wine and of vintners.

Bonfires were lighted on the eve of his day, and animals that could not be fed through the winter were slaughtered and salted down. Perhaps in memory of older winter sacrifices, their blood was sometimes sprinkled on their owners' thresholds. Saint Martin's Day was one of feasting, when the first of the new wine was drunk. And in memory of his patronage, German children placed vessels of water on their doorsteps with the plea that the water be changed to wine. On the morning of Martinmas, the water would indeed be wine; beside it would lie a special cookie, shaped like a horseshoe to show that the saint had ridden by in the night.

Saint Andrew's Day

November 30, Saint Andrew's Day, was a
holiday in Scotland, in Central Europe and in
Greece. For the Scots, it was a day when
squirrels were traditionally hunted and eaten at
feasts. Farther south, the eve of the day
was one of prophecy, when maidens might see
in dreams the men they were to marry. And
in Rumania, the eve was the time when the dead
were freed and vampires haunted countryside
and village. Doorjambs were hung with garlic
then, to keep the specters away, and no
wise person ventured out on the highways, for
at the crossroads the ghostly creatures fought
among themselves until dawn.

Saint Nicholas' Day

When the old gods ruled the world, Odin the All-father rode the skies of Germany and Scandinavia in winter with a crowd of elves and spirits; those mortals who offered him reverence were rewarded with gifts. In later years, Odin's horse, elves and gifts became the accouterments of a Christian saint named Nicholas.

Nicholas lived in Asia Minor. Because he calmed storms at sea during his life, he became the patron of sailors; and because he restored to life three murdered youths, he became the patron of boys. But the most famous tale concerning him was that of three maidens whose impoverished father planned to sell them into slavery. Nicholas redeemed them with three bags of dowry gold, which he flung through their windows one night and which landed on their shoes, set to warm before the fire. For this deed, he became the patron of maidens, and Frenchwomen prayed to him for husbands.

He also became the patron of pawnbrokers, and his bags of gold are remembered in the three golden balls that are the sign of the trade. But gift-giving was his most important act. In Germany and Holland, children set out their shoes on the eve of his feast day, filling them with hay and carrots for his white horse, just as provender had been left for Odin's horse by their ancestors. Nicholas, they knew, would ride over the rooftops in the night with his elvish companion, Knecht Ruprecht. Ruprecht carried a switch for use on naughty young ones. But Nicholas carried baskets of toys and sweets, to be left in the shoes of all good children.

Saint Lucia's Day

In the countries of the north, where winter darkness held longest, people's yearning for light found focus on the feast day of Saint Lucia of Sicily, whose very name, they thought, meant light. That day was December 13, which in early calendars marked the winter solstice. When calendars were reformed, the solstice fell on December 21, but the feast of Lucia continued to mark the beginning of Christmas in Sweden and in Norway.

Old folk said that on the eve of the day, Lucia herself might be seen, skimming across the snowfields and frozen lakes, a crown of light upon her hair. In the towns, torchlight processions were held to summon back the luminescence that had withered away. And the daughters of each house rose in the early dark, dressed in white, crowned with wreaths of lingonberry or holly and blazing candles, they would take food and fire to their sleeping elders, singing all the while to mark the morning of Saint Lucia's Day.

The Day of the Solstice

From time before memory, people danced to make magic, and throughout Europe, they danced at the solstice as a defense against the dark. The recollection of those early ceremonies lived on in the form of village sword dances, performed on the shortest of days, December 21. Clothed in elaborate ribboned costumes, men would circle sunwise – from left to right, in the apparent path of the sun – using the swords they bore to form patterns in the air. The most important pattern marked the climax of the dance: It was a six-pointed star, the earthly symbol of the longed-for sun.

Christmas Eve

Christmas Eve was a time for human feasting — and for something else. In Scandinavia, people said, the ghosts of the dead returned in the night to visit the homes they had loved. Their descendants welcomed them: After the meal of the living was finished, food was left for the dead. Then the living retired, so their ancestors might come into the warmth and the light to make their old Christmas revels once more.

Christmas Day

As midnight ushered in the day of Christmas, tranquillity descended on all the world, according to the old tales. Even in the darkness, all the birds awoke and sang, and such was the magic of the time that sparrows caroled as sweetly as nightingales. In the morning, men and women who walked into the wildernesses of the world might see all the beasts of field and wood lying placidly together, predator and prey joined for one day to make a peaceable kingdom.

New Year's Eve

In order that the New Year might prosper, the old year – and the spirits released by the solstice season – had to be buried or driven away. In villages from Britain to Austria, the old year – in the form of a straw dummy called Death – was carried through the streets and then drowned in a stream or buried or burned. But other people in other villages had more high-spirited customs. On New Year's Eve, costumed and masked as a disguise against malevolent powers, people paraded through their towns, striking the houses with sticks, beating drums, clanging bells and cracking whips. The noise of the "town rattling," as it was called, drove out the ghosts of the dying old year and brought the New Year safely in.

Twelfth Night

The eve of the twelfth day of Christmas once was the time for ensuring the health of growing things that had been sent to sleep by the winter. In the west of England on that night, farmers trooped into their orchards to take wassail – good health – to their apple trees. The apple tree, long revered for its fruit, was thought to house its own elfin spirit. With songs and shouts, the men called upon the tree to awaken from its sleep. One reveler would be masked as a bull, symbol of fertility. And all made offerings to the tree's spirit to ensure its fruitfulness: In a fork of its branches, they placed bread and salt, or sometimes a cake soaked in cider from the wassail bowl. The branches themselves were dipped in cider or sprinkled with it in libation.

Brigit's Day

The British of ancient times had a goddess of youth and fertility named Bride; Christians called her Saint Brigit and celebrated her feast on February 1. But the celebrations were far older than Christianity. Bride, the folk said, was held prisoner during the dark months in the mountain of the goddess of winter, who used a silver hammer to cover the earth with ice. At the beginning of February, the young goddess was released. On the eve of the feast day in Ireland and Scotland, people set candles burning to summon the returning light of spring, which followed in Bride's footsteps. They then placed a bed by the threshold and called a welcome into the darkness. When morning came, they examined the ashes in the hearth. Signs of disturbance there were a good omen: They meant that Bride was once more abroad in the land and that winter had been driven away.

II

THE HEART OF DARKNESS

On a Christmas night centuries ago, a curious scene was played out against a winter landscape in southern England. The snow was thick, resting in curving ridges on the branches, rising pillow-like on the roofs of a sleeping village. All the land was white and silent, quietly shining back to the stars. But the wrapping of winter hid old secrets. Some villagers were stirring long after the church bells had tolled midnight.

Lights appeared at cottage doors and moved through the narrow streets, clustering by the well. The lights were cressets—small oil lamps shielded from the night wind by lantern frames of iron and horn—and the people who held them were young men, walking in Christmas guise: Their faces were blackened with soot; their bodies were bundled against the cold; and along with their lanterns, they carried poles and cudgels. Jostling and laughing, they left the well and trudged through the snow, past the houses, past the church, past the sheepfolds and cow byres huddled at the edge of the village, onto the path that led to the empty winter fields.

By the time morning's first light shone red on the hills, the men were far from their houses. They could be seen as dark figures moving in the hedgerows, beating at the bare branches of hawthorn and blackthorn with their poles, so that the small birds hidden within the tangle tumbled frantically up in an effort to escape.

It was a small bird that the men hunted. They were the Wren Boys of Christmas, seeking a wren for the village. He who managed to flush one from its hiding place and break its fragile back with a blow of his staff became their King for that day.

The King was the master of the ceremony. He placed the tiny creature on a miniature bier hung with ribbons and mounted on a pole. Then he led his fellows down the track and back toward the village, where smoke from the morning fires curled out of the chimneys.

As they neared the houses, the Wren Boys grew raucous, shouting their triumph and laughing at the cold. Shutters flew open and rosy faces peered out. At the first house, the young men halted at the gate and caroled a nonsense song:

We hunted the wren for Robin the Bobbin,
We hunted the wren for Jack of the Can,
We hunted the wren for Robin the Bobbin,
We hunted the wren for every man.

At the final note, the cottage door flew open. In the entry stood the housewife, grinning, waving a present for the Wren Boys: a tankard of steaming ale. The men

passed the ale around; the King plucked a ruddy feather from the bird and presented it with a flourish to the housewife.

After that, the Wren Boys trooped from house to house, singing their odd song, taking their gifts, presenting their feathers. When all the houses of the village had been visited, the young men changed their melody to a dirge. They carried the wren to the churchyard, where they dug a little grave for it and laid it in the earth.

With variations, this scene once took place in villages and towns all around Europe—sometimes on Christmas morning, sometimes on December 26, Saint Stephen's Day, sometimes on New Year's Day, sometimes at Epiphany. On the Isle of Man, the bird was carried not on a bier but suspended by its legs from the intersection of two crossed hoops that were decorated with evergreen boughs and ribbons; the feathers were given  to Manx fishermen as a charm against shipwreck. In France, the wren was slung beneath a carrying pole and the King of the Wren Boys was crowned and treated as royalty—with torchlight processions and feasting—all through the Christmas season. Some Wren Boys carried the prize in a garlanded wren house with glass sides. The Irish tied the bird to an uprooted holly bush bedecked with streamers. No matter what the details, the intent was always the same: The killing of the wren and the distribution of its feathers brought good health and good fortune to the villagers.

But why should the killing of a tiny bird bring luck? And why, particularly, the wren, that pretty hedge dweller with its fluting, sparkling song? Indeed, the wren had been from time immemorial the most sacred of birds, and its divinity was commemorated in names: In Latin, the bird was called *regulus*, or "little king"; in German, *Zaunkönig*, or "hedge king," and *Schneekönig*, meaning "snow king"; the French named it *poulet de Dieu*, which means "God's chicken." On every day of the year but one, the harming of a wren was sacrilege, sure to bring misfortune. Scotsmen said that if a wren were harmed, cows would give bloody milk. And in France, those who robbed wrens' nests risked their houses, which might burn down, or their fingers, which might shrivel and fall off as punishment. To show their affection for the bird, the French liked to tell of an early saint who laid his habit on a bush while he labored in his monastery's vineyard. A wren built its nest there, and the saint, rather than disturb it, did without his habit until the nestlings had flown.

Why the wren was revered no one could say for certain. The bird frequents dark places—thickets, crevices—and therefore, perhaps, partook of the powers that resided in the earth. Some people said that the wren was the bird that first brought fire to earth from heaven; it was scorched by the sun, which gave its feathers their reddish tinge. Others told the tale of a dispute for sovereignty among birds: The crown was to be given to the one that could fly closest to the sun. The eagle outsoared them all, but a wren, which had hidden in the eagle's feathers, leaped out at the crest of the flight and so flew higher, defeating the eagle and winning the crown.

Whatever the reason, the bird was wreathed in mystery and endowed with power; its life was precious. By a logic rooted deep in the human mind, it was therefore a candidate for sacrifice.

The hunting of the wren, although the hunters could not have said why, was a sacrifice, an echo of winter rituals practiced since the time when humans first conceived the notion of gods. The sacred bird's death was a gift to the powers of the universe and a plea for favor and good fortune; the sharing of its feathers linked the mortals to the divine.

In the earliest times, kings served as the link. Sovereigns were sacred: The fertility of the land depended upon them. And in some countries, after a reign of a year—or eight years, or whenever famine threatened—the kings were sacrificed for their people, and their flesh was sown in the fields to ensure fertility. Most cultures propitiated the gods in less drastic ways, however. They sacrificed animals thought to hold mystic power: the bull, the horse, the boar. People ate the flesh of these beasts to share communion with divinity; they masked themselves in the skulls and skins to partake of the animals' strength and fecundity.

Long after the old religions had been displaced, the memory of winter sacrifices lived on in Christmas customs. Some rituals, like the hunting of the wren, showed their ancestry quite clearly. In parts of Ireland, for instance, it was the custom at Christmas to slaughter a bird—a chicken, a goose—for the Christmas feast and sprinkle a few drops of its blood on the thresh-

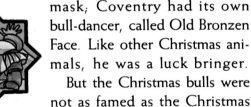

old of the house for luck. The Scots went hunting on New Year's Day, and the blood of the first animal killed ensured good fortune for the killer.

Most relics of sacrificial customs were distant from their sanguinary origins. They took the form of processions of people in disguise, and they were full of merriment; only the faintest tinge of the solemnity of old ritual remained. When the Romans ruled Britain, for instance, the soldiers of the legions that followed Mithra, god of light, sacrificed bulls to him. Centuries later, all that remained of the religion were comical Christmas maskers, such as the Ooser of Dorset, who paraded the villages disguised with a bull's mask; Coventry had its own bull-dancer, called Old Bronzen Face. Like other Christmas animals, he was a luck bringer.

But the Christmas bulls were not as famed as the Christmas hobbyhorses, descendants of the ceremonies of the coldest north. In Viking Norway, wrote the chroniclers, midwinter feasts were held this way: The warriors would come from their strongholds, down snowy hills by sled and ski, bringing casks of ale and grain and driving before them horses and sheep. Into their chieftain's hall they would crowd, lining the long central hearth. There, before the image of the All-father, Odin, their horses would die under the knife. The blood of the animals, gathered in bowls, was sprinkled over the pedestal before the god's figure, over the floor of the hall, over the heads of the people. A cup of the blood was passed from hand to hand, and when all had

drunk from it, the feasting proper began.

Recollections of this sacrifice far outlasted the Vikings. For centuries, it was the custom in Britain—a country that had endured long years of Viking rule—to bleed horses (but not to kill them) on Saint Stephen's Day. The bleeding was thought to cleanse the animals. But the day chosen for the ritual, the heart of winter, requires another explanation, the most likely being a chain of links to ancient horse sacrifices.

The connection to the old gods was more obvious in the British Christmas ritual called hodening. To those who took part, it seemed a riotous jape that might, at the worst, frighten the more impressionable onlookers. The central figure was a man concealed in a horse blanket or sheet, from the top of which the head of a horse protruded. It could be a wooden head, sometimes gaudily painted, or it could be a real horse's skull. In either case, a contrivance of wire was used to make the jaws snap open and shut in a threatening way, and candles were often set into the eyes to make them glow. This "hoden" was accompanied through the streets of its town, sometimes by a driver, who held the horse's reins, sometimes by pipers and drummers. Other men, with no specific role to play, would join the procession. Children would try to mount the horse, women would run from it. All would toss gifts of sweets or money into the snapping mouth and petition the animal for luck.

The hoden, stomping and charging and bucking in the streets, was plainly a survival of some ancient horse rite. A clue to its ancestry survives in its name. The word "hodening" has been linked with the horse-shaped hood that covered the head of the principal actor, and with wood, from which the head was sometimes made. But it has been traced with more authority to the name of the Norse god to whom horses were sacrificed: Odin.

Sacrifice and the echoes of sacrifice lingered so long in winter celebrations because winter's threat to humankind was great. In Britain and in countries farther north, it seemed that the world died each year with the light. The very stars that ruled the lives of mortals were ranked in cruel array, the astrologers said. Along the belt of constellations that formed the zodiac reigned baleful Scorpio—the scorpion that fought against the sun. A demon creature, sometimes called the "Lurking One," it was the font of death and darkness. Sagittarius, the Archer, forever pursued it, his arrow aimed at the scorpion's starry heart, yet never slew the ancient monster. And behind Sagittarius, mercurial and shifty, came Capricorn: the goatfish, author of chaos.

In the wildernesses of the earth, it seemed that the old gods—those who were remembered only in superstition and ritual—were stirring, heaving up their hoary heads to observe with anger the puny intruders on their ancient territories. In Scotland, in Ireland and in Wales, winter was the time of the hag goddess, known in Gaelic as Cailleac Bheur, or Old Wife: She rose from her place of concealment in a rock or a mountain to entrap Bride, the spirit of spring. In Scandinavia, the forests and snowfields trembled as encroaching darkness awoke the eldest of all gods. These were the *brim-thursar*, or

Stamping his feet, tossing his head, the man who played the hodening horse
pranced through British streets and brought luck to all. The "hoden" was a jolly Christmas creature, but its past was dark: It was a relic of ancient winter sacrifice.

"frost giants." Kari, the wind that blew down from the mountains and in from the sea, was the first among them. Kari was father of Frosti, the frost, who in turn sired a snow giantess and a brood of snow-gods. All of them together constituted winter, drifting secretly into hall and town, reaching cold fingers through window and door, shrouding the forest, strangling the fields.

The people did what they could in the face of the threat. In November, when the season began to turn and the days to draw in, when dry leaves rattled on tree branches and the stubbled pastures lay stiff with frost, men and women slaughtered the animals they could not feed through the winter; the Anglo-Saxons referred to November as Blood Month for this reason. Custom assigned certain days to slaughtering. In England, Saint Martin's Day, November 11, was set aside for the killing of cattle, to produce the traditional Martinmas beef; in Germany, the animals slaughtered on that day were swine, hens and geese. In the Orkney Islands, December 17, Saint Ignace's Day, was the day for killing pigs and so was called Sow Day.

Nor were the fruits of the field neglected. At the end of the harvest, the last sheaf of grain — barley, rye or wheat — was always carefully saved, as was the straw made from the grain stalks, for the very spirit of the field lived in these plants. Treasuring them ensured a good harvest for the coming year. In Sweden and Denmark, the grain from the last sheaf was made into a Christmas cake; in parts of England, it yielded a frumenty, a sweet porridge that, when eaten on Christmas morning, con-

ferred the health of growing things on men and women. In Staffordshire and Yorkshire, among other places, the stalks of the last sheaf were woven into a corn dolly ("corn" being the term for grain), which might be shaped as a tree, or a man, or a bird or a goat. This was hung in the house during the season to bless the household, then fed to the cattle in the byre, to bless them, too. As for the straw, it was strewn on house floor and church floor and on barren fields to strengthen them.

Yet the efforts of the people — their sacrifices, their corn dollies, the evergreen branches they kept to recall growing things, the fires they set to summon back the sun — seemed of little avail at the depth of the season. Then men and women huddled in their halls and houses, getting what warmth and light they could from their hearth fires and their rushlights, while outside the old gods roamed free, accompanied by the host of darkness — by goblins and fairies and, worst of all, by ghosts.

This was the season of the dead. The Norse Yule, with its sacrifices and its feasting, occurred near the solstice, but it had its beginnings as a festival of the dead, made to honor the ancestors of the people, pale shades released by the hiding of the sun, who drifted in along the shore if they had died at sea, or rose from the funeral barrows that held them in the earth. Out of their hidden worlds they came, to visit once more the world of the living.

Even when Christianity and its rituals had absorbed and gentled the Yule celebration, people remembered the old gods and said that they returned to claim the human dead. When the winter wind

Astrologers said the fate of the winter-born was hidden in the constellations clustered along the zodiac. There ruled cruel Scorpio, hunted by the Archer, Sagittarius, with Capricorn the goat-fish cavorting close behind.

From the ancient breath of Kari, the winter wind, descended cold No

ds: *Black Frost, Eternal Snowbank, Snowdrift, Fine-driven Snow.*

howled outside, filling the world with cloud and snow, the folk of the northern lands heard the mighty shout of Odin, hunting the skies with a wild band of lost and hungry souls. It was death to Christians to see this Jolerei, or "Yuletide Host." Wise folk kept safe in their houses.

The ghostly hunting band of Christmas had other names in other places. In the north of England, it was known as the Gabriel hounds or the Gabriel rache, meaning "corpse hounds"—fiery-eyed ghost dogs that rode the clouds. Sometimes King Arthur was said to be their leader. In Wales, the huntsman was known as Gwyn ap Nudd, King of the underworld. And in parts of Germany, the hunter was an elder goddess—Berchta, who traveled the earth with elves and fairies and with the ghosts of tiny children. (In Christian times, Berchta survived in the world of humble folk. She cherished the souls of infants who had died unbaptized and so forfeited the protection of the Church.) The goddess rode over farm and cottage, examining the barns for cleanliness, judging the distaffs and spindles of the housewives. Hearths were swept clean for her inspection. Houses were adorned with evergreens. Pancakes were left out for her to eat. Cakes were baked in the shape of slippers that could be filled with small presents the goddess left behind.

If she was not fed or if the households were untidy and unthrifty, Berchta sent plagues and mutilations; if people spied on her activities, she blinded them. But the goddess had a gentler side.

According to a tale told in the Tyrol, she showed great generosity toward a farmer who, against all wisdom, ventured outdoors on Epiphany Eve. With his lantern in his hand, he walked through his own stableyard that night: He had drunk deep of Yule ale, and the cold air refreshed him. He stopped in his tracks, however, when he heard the sound of high voices singing and calling. White figures moved among the stars: Berchta was aloft.

Swiftly she descended, alighting with her train of infant ghosts. The company flitted through the farmer's barn and across the stableyard. Berchta swept past the farmer, apparently unseeing, and he shivered as the cold mist of her robe brushed his arm. Little figures tumbled after her like so many chicks, chattering in light voices. But one of them lagged behind, a toddler in a long nightshirt that clung to his feet and upset his uncertain balance, so that, every few steps, he fell clumsily onto the cold earth. The farmer, a father himself, acted with rough kindness. He picked up the little ghost and held him steady with one hand, while with the other he bound his own garter around the belly to serve as a belt that would hold up the nightshirt. Then he set the creature on his feet and gave a little push to send him in the goddess's direction.

Berchta stood on the farmer's threshold, observing. She smiled when the ghost reached her, and her old eyes were gay. "A kind man," she said. "My blessings on your own children. They shall never want." And so it was. The farmer's children enjoyed long lives, and good ones.

Such simple tales were told of Berchta when her ancient powers had been weakened by new beliefs. But once she had

Old gods haunted the winter skies of Europe, terrifying men and women. In Germany, the hearth goddess Berchta rode the clouds, leading a train of elves and fairies, cradling the ghosts of the infant dead.

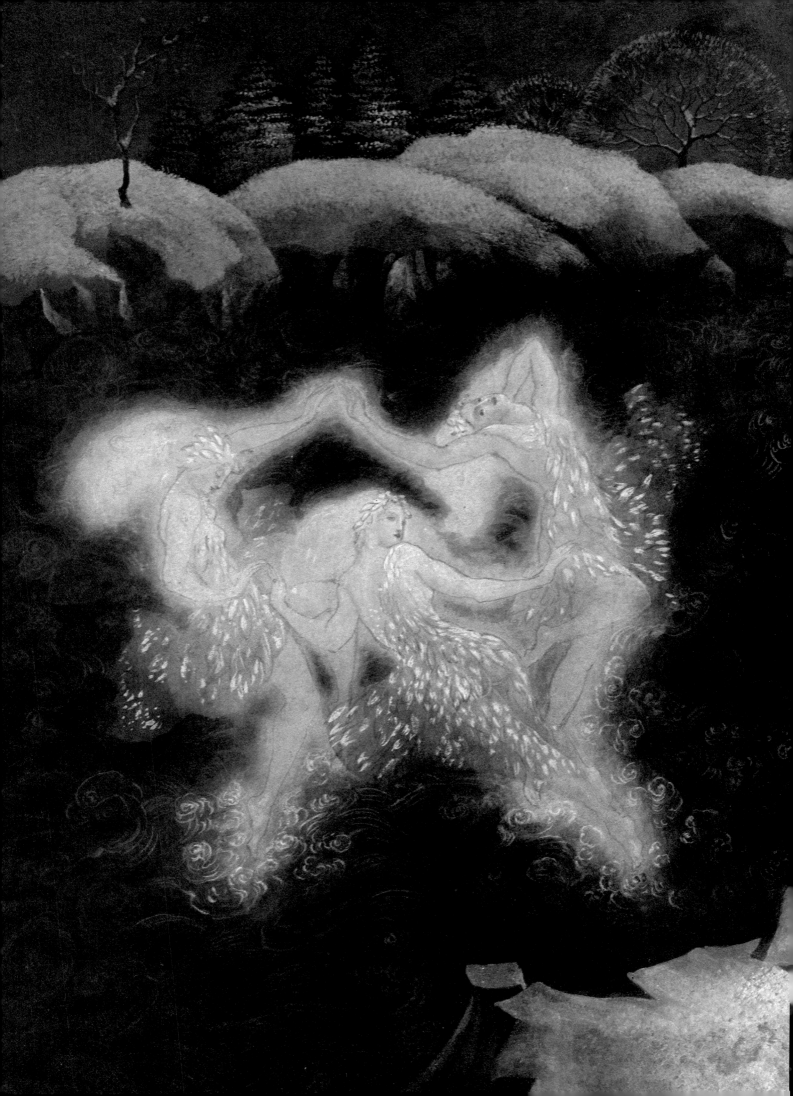

The magic of the twelve Christmas days freed the spirits
of field, wood and water. In Russian forests, nymphs called rusalky left their
lakes and streams to dance and sing their secret songs.

Out of rocks and caves, out of the solid earth itself, came goblins the Greeks called callicantzari, who tormented honest households where Christmas feasts were held.

been the premier goddess of the hearth and the guardian of the household. In pagan days, the Yuletide season was the time when an altar of flat stone was made for Berchta in each house; upon this altar burned a fire of evergreen boughs. Berchta could be called up from the wood smoke, to rise among the flames and tell the future of each one present at her hearth.

The chance to transcend time was one of the wonderful – if ambiguous – offerings of the solstice darkness; at that pivotal moment, folk might see into the past and glimpse the days to come. Innumerable ceremonies existed for the purpose; they were staged on Saint Andrew's Eve, Christmas Eve, New Year's Eve and Twelfth Night. A maiden would sleep with pieces of bread under her pillow, for instance; if, in the morning, the bread was found partly eaten, the maiden's lover would marry her before the following year was out. Omens were to be found in the Yule straw brought from the last harvest into a Norwegian house. The grains that fell from it signified not only what crops should be planted in the spring, but also – by their health or lack of health – whether the crops would be large ones. If the grains were discovered under a chair on Christmas morning, the person sitting in that chair would die in the new year. The most powerful omens, however, were given by those who walked free in the heart of darkness: goddesses such as Berchta, who might be petitioned for prophecy, and the ghosts who rode in their trains.

These Christmas ghosts entered the houses of their descendants to feast on the offerings left for them and make merry in the night; during Christian times, they also held their own Christmas ceremonies. They gathered in deserted churches at midnight on Christmas Eve. To see them was dangerous, because they were eager for mortals to join their tattered company and because they had a following: The fetches – or doubles – of folk doomed to die trailed behind, as if longing to see the companions who would soon join them.

This would seem to have been a good reason for avoiding churches in the Christmas hours when Christians slept and the churches were empty. Yet human curiosity often overrode human fear. There were some who braved the churchyards for the sake of forbidden knowledge. One of these was a parish priest of the village of Walton-le-Dale in Lancashire. He was an unassuming man, courteous enough to his parishioners, but he was solitary, a student of oddities who sought to learn the qualities of plants and the secrets of the stars. He had the habit of talking to himself, which made his flock fear him. They said that he spoke with devils.

He had only one companion, an elderly herb doctor known as Old Abraham. This was the man who told the priest's tale.

One Christmas Eve, after the services were over and the people had gone to their homes, the priest persuaded Old Abraham to watch with him by the church door to see the ghosts of the folk about to die as they wandered in the night. Abraham agreed readily. He had taught the priest his lore, and he was quite willing to see into the future. Near midnight then, the two men crept through the quiet village to the little yard where the church stood. The

At Christmas, the future was revealed: A man
might see the shades of those who would die in the new year. But
among them, he might also see himself.

A winter crone called Frau Gaude crept at Christmastide into Austrian
villages, leading her pack of demon dogs. Woe to the families whose doors were left open: Frau Gaude
sent her dogs in and nothing could drive the beasts away.

place was quiet: No ghosts watched there. On the church altar, a single taper burned. In the churchyard, the moon shone silver on stone and branch.

The men settled in the shadow of the church porch, wrapping their coats around them. Drawing on Abraham's knowledge of the virtues of plants, they had provided themselves with protection. They carried sprigs of St.-John's-wort, the summer flower used in prognostication and as a guard against ghosts; bay leaf, which was the herb of the sun and a defense against the devil and the dark; holly, the evergreen whose red berries warded off evil; and mountain ash, descendant of the world tree from which, according to the old herbalist, the first man was made.

The moments rolled by; so still was the churchyard that the rustlings of small animals that hunted by night were clearly audible. Beyond the wall, where the woods began, an owl hooted. Then the wind rose and sighed in the tree branches; somewhere, a bell tolled. At the sound, movement began in the churchyard, an aimless fluttering movement, as of shadows flicked by the wind. A figure glided along the path. The face was well-known to the priest and Old Abraham: It was that of the miller of the town. Behind him walked others the two men knew: the midwife, the schoolmaster, a farmer. These four shuffled by the watchers on the church porch, looking neither left nor right; as they passed the men, they faded into shadow.

The priest sighed, curiosity satisfied. Then he gasped, and as Old Abraham was later to explain, he had good reason. The last walker in the ghostly company was the priest himself; the specter looked up as it passed the porch and gave a tight smile. That was the man's reward for meddling with winter magic: He died within the year, having foreseen his own demise.

Most people were more cautious than he, wary of the ghosts that walked at Christmas, fearing the spirits of the earth that were freed to wander then. In the wild places, these spirits slipped the bonds of tree, of rock, of lake and brook to ride upon the winter wind and dance in the snow. In Russia, for instance, the *rusalky* – sometimes said to be the ghosts of young women, sometimes water fairies – emerged from streams and rivers to dance and sing. They were clothed in green leaves and crowned with starlit hair; they sang of all that was past or passing or to come. But it was a danger for mortals to hear them: Men and women who ventured out on winter nights risked their sanity. The song of the *rusalky* took the soul away.

These spirits kept to their woodland fastnesses, however. Other Christmas creatures went seeking humankind. In Rumania, werewolves prowled during the twelve nights; in Greece, goblins called *callicantzari* nipped out from under rocks and from within mountain caves and scampered, chattering and gibbering, to the towns where people lived. Down the chimneys they would slide, wreaking havoc in any household they invaded, befouling the Christmas feast, riding the shoulders of the householders, pinching and pulling at the children. Sometimes these grotesqueries were said to be spirits of the dead; sometimes they were thought to be children who had been born at Christmas

Among Iceland's destructive winter spirits were the Christmas Lad

...rteen trolls who invaded farms, took food and stole the children.

and were vulnerable to the transforming spells of the old ones. To ward off the *callicantzari*, Greeks would hang in the fireplace the jawbone of a pig, which was thought to have protective powers. Most important of all, they would keep their Christmas fires burning all during the season; often, the fires were made from fruit trees and were sprinkled with dried fruits. The earthbound sun kept the dark ones away.

Christmas was full of old elves who descended on human towns and created mischief. Germans told of one called Frau Gaude, a descendant of the goddess Berchta, some said. At Christmas, accompanied by a pack of demon dogs, she would steal into the villages and search for careless householders who had left their doors ajar. When she found such a house, she would send in a dog to crouch by the hearth, whining steadily. Nothing would make it go away. If the householders killed it, the dog would take on the innocuous form of a rock. At night, it would awaken and whine again, bringing illness and misfortune to the house. It disappeared only when another Christmas had come and the year's spell had run its course.

A few of the elder creatures that haunted the world wrought terrible evil—or so the stories say: They were child-stealers. Among these were the Christmas Lads of Iceland, thirteen in all, who descended on Icelandic households one at a time, beginning thirteen days before Christmas. They were the sons of an ancient she-troll called Gryla; they stole candles and sausage, took away the good grain, wrecked the tidy Christmas rooms. One by one they left again, beginning on Christmas Day, and when they left, they took away the children of the house, stuffed in sacks.

According to the tales, the children they took were the naughty ones—which suggests that the Christmas Lads were chimerical, only a threat that parents used to ensure the good behavior of their excited offspring during the festive season. The same is probably true of other reported child-stealers. For instance, Laplanders told of a predatory mountain troll named Stalo. Seeking human flesh, this creature would come creeping down into settlements during the longest nights of winter and steal away small boys who dared to leave their houses to ski in the moonlit snow. But Stalo was an old troll, easily defeated, even by children, as the children themselves would tell. They said he captured a company of them once, stuffed them in his sack and dragged them toward his mountain lair. But Stalo set the sack down when he paused to rest. The children quickly crawled out, then put rocks in their place so that the troll would not detect their absence. The last that was seen of him was a crooked shadow, toiling slowly up a mountainside, dragging the rocks behind him. As for the children, they ran home, where a cross was painted on the door to keep the old winter spirits out, where the evergreens hung, happily alive in the dead of winter, where the straw of the harvest coated the floor, promising health and plenty, where the Yule log burned, keeping back the dark and conferring blessing on the household, the promise that the sun would return again and with its light bring joy.

No matter how stern the ogres of winter, they could be defeated by guile or luck.
So some Lapp children, stolen by the giant Stalo, escaped from his sack, leaving stones in their places.
The giant dragged the sack to his lair, while the children ran home.

The Midnight Battle

The enchantments of deep winter were once as myriad and various as snowflakes. Freed by the dark season, beings of the other world floated on the night wind through the streets of towns and made their way into houses. These elvish spirits offered curious and tempting delights, but their gifts were wrapped in peril, as a German tale reveals:

Its unfolding began on a Christmas Eve in Nuremberg long years ago, when twilight settled on the town, leaving the snow-thatched roofs to shine white above empty, muffled streets. All good folk were safe in their homes, out of the bitter dark. The windows were yellow rectangles of firelight and candlelight, and the adults of the households moved in and out of view, bearing green garlands and bright decorations as they fashioned the holiday for their children.

Through the shadowy hall of one house, a small figure hobbled, a crooked, white-haired, gnomelike fellow who clutched an enormous box. With a glance around from his one good eye (the other eye was covered by a large black patch), he pushed open the door of a parlor, letting out light and music for a moment; then he vanished inside, closing the door firmly behind him. When the old man had gone, footsteps sounded on the staircase that led down to the hall, as those who had watched for him stole down to the parlor door. One of the watchers was a maiden just out of girlhood; the other was a much younger boy. Both were pale with excitement – and perhaps with fear. Wreathed in the scents of Christmas – of

On Christmas Eve, in a house in Nuremberg mantled by snow, the children Fritz and Marie waited for the lights of Christmas and the magic made by Drosselmeier the clockmaker.

cinnamon and burnt sugar, of pine branch and wood smoke—they waited by the door. With infinite attention, they listened to the rise and fall of voices in the parlor, to the snatches of music that floated out, to the crackle of paper, to tappings and rustlings.

The master of that house in Nuremberg was called Stahlbaum, and the watchers by his parlor door were Marie and Fritz, his children. The little old man was their godfather, Drosselmeier, a clockmaker of more than mortal skill, a provider of presents that lived by enchantment: of miniature men that could smile and bow as prettily as any courtier, of birds no larger than beans that could sing as sweetly as any summer lark, of puppets that danced at Drosselmeier's will and wooden soldiers that marched at his command. The parents said these treasures were marvels of the clockmaker's art, too fragile even to touch except at Christmas, so that during the year the toys were locked away. But the children understood that the creatures were quickened by Drosselmeier's magic; the nature of the toys was such that only at the heart of Christmas did they live, and only by his hand were they set free.

Marie and Fritz therefore waited quietly in the hall, while the evening gloom gave way to night and the moon rose above the town, shining coldly on them through a window. At last, a bell chimed high and silver; the voices behind the door grew closer and louder, and then the door opened to let the children into Christmas.

They paused on the threshold, caught in wonder. The room was bathed in golden light, the nimbus of a hundred candles. Against one wall, rising proudly from its table to the ceiling, stood the Christmas tree, its tapers sparkling, as if all the stars of winter had been trapped in its green branches to illuminate the fruits of summer that hung among the boughs—apples of silver and gold, buds made of sugared

Under the clockmaker's eye the Christmas revels proceeded, and in his enchanted castle, miniature people reveled, too. Fritz played with an army of soldiers; Marie cradled a nutcracker.

almonds, marzipan flowers, gilded nuts and berries. On the table, a squadron of hussars, armed with silver swords, sat in ranks on motionless horses that seemed just at the edge of life. And all around lay ribboned packages, wrapped in mystery.

Over all this, Drosselmeier presided, crouched spider-like by the table. A man of few words, he said nothing while Fritz and Marie smiled and exclaimed and opened their gifts. But presently, when the dancing began and the adults were occupied, he caught the children's eye and gestured toward a corner of the room. There, in a glass cabinet, the inventions of former years—dolls, toy soldiers, carved animals—stared down upon the wonder Drosselmeier had made.

Rising from the floor to half the room's height was a castle from a fairy tale, a many-windowed and many-towered palace. When the children gazed upon it, bells pealed from the towers and the windows flew open, showing splendid rooms within. In a long gallery lined with mirrors, tiny, silk-robed courtiers promenaded slowly to and fro, bowing and smiling to one another, speaking in tones as high and light as the singing of distant birds. Another window revealed a grand hall, lighted by chandeliers in which countless tapers burned; the candle flames were no larger than grains of wheat, but they served to illuminate the elfin children who danced beneath. At one portal, a man appeared, staring out at the watching children. A bent, elderly creature, he wore a white wig and a black eye patch. He was the miniature image of Drosselmeier. After a moment, he gave a crooked grin and withdrew into his tower.

Entranced, the children peered into the windows of the castle at the apparently living dolls. But young Fritz grew restive: Could he be sent into the small world, he wanted to know; could the dolls be made to come out; would they dance a different

Before midnight, the nutcracker was laid away. The lights were dimmed. The young ones were led to their bedchambers. And Drosselmeier watched it all and smiled a secret smile.

dance? To Fritz's questions, Drosselmeier always answered that the patterns were set and could not be altered. Fritz stumped away to play with his toy soldiers, whose patterns could be altered, and by him. After a while, Marie too left the enchanted castle to walk among the living dancers and examine again the glittering tree. She settled beside it, cradling in her arms a present Drosselmeier had made for her.

This was a small creature, its young man's body clothed, like Fritz's soldiers, in the braid-trimmed jacket, pantaloons and boots of a hussar. Its enormous, slack-jawed, large-toothed head sat oddly on that slender frame; glass eyes set in the grotesque face stared out at the world with an expression of thoughtful melancholy. Those eyes gave the creature a life not its own. It was, in fact, a particularly fanciful nutcracker; its great jaw, pushed by a lever concealed in its back, was meant for crushing shells.

A little too old for dolls, Marie nevertheless caressed this one, feeding a nut to it from time to time, until she attracted her brother's attention. Fritz was overtired. His face, flushed and sweaty, was smeared with crumbs and sugar crystals; his voice had risen to an irritating whine. He demanded the nutcracker; when he had it, he thrust an enormous hazelnut into its mouth and hammered at the lever. With an appalling crack, the wooden joint separated, and the nut rolled out. Fritz stared at the broken device, his mouth pursed and his red face wrinkling; he threw the nutcracker to the floor and let out a howl of temper that brought his elders to his side. Within moments he was carried off by his nurse, still crying.

The outburst seemed to signal the end of the magic; indeed, the hour was late. While Marie picked her nutcracker up, turning it about in her hands, her parents and their companions moved about the parlor, snuffing candles; the maids ar-

When the house was asleep, Marie returned for the nutcracker. As she entered the room, the clock chimed midnight at Drosselmeier's command, summoning the mouse army that ruled the dark.

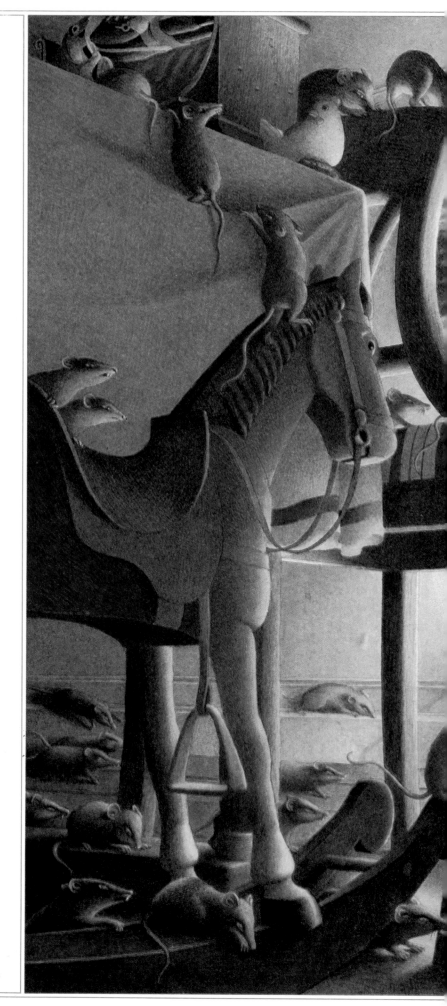

rived to clear away the food. One by one, the people left the room, until Marie was alone with her parents and Drosselmeier. He said, quite kindly, "Bind the wound; all will be well come morning." At his words, the nutcracker's face seemed to twist into a snarl. But that was no more than a trick of the light. Marie wrapped her handkerchief about the creature's head to hold its jaw in place and put it in a doll's bed left beside the tree. Then her mother led her away. She glanced back once. Drosselmeier remained in the parlor, muttering over his castle.

An hour later, when the house slept, Marie slipped into the parlor. The place was shadowy and still; the eyes of the toy beings in their glass cupboard looked out on shapes illumined only by the dying glow of a single candle. By the tree table, tiny hussars ranged in ranks. Above them, the nutcracker lay motionless on its pillows, sheltered by green boughs.

Marie stepped across the threshold and paused, listening. The clock on the mantle, loudly ticking, gave a whirring rumble and began to chime the stroke of midnight. As if in answer, from every corner of the room came scratchings and clicks and rustlings. The walls themselves were waking. The shadows shifted and wriggled all around, stretching and shrinking. Tiny lights winked in them, here and there.

A settling movement caught the maiden's eye, and she turned. Something perched on the clock—a great bird, whose wings mantled the clock's hands. It raised its head and grinned at her, a manic, gleaming grin. It was Drosselmeier, shrunk small. What she had taken for wings were the folds of his cloak.

With a cry, Marie leaped away, but too late. The entire room was in motion. Every table, every chair, every picture frame swarmed with mice, scuttling and scampering, twitching their heads this way and that. Across the floor they tumbled, a

The mice grew and Marie shrank, leaving her helpless against their power. But Christmas engendered benign enchantment, too: The Nutcracker sprang to life, calling soldiers to battle.

flood of vermin rolling toward Marie.

Suddenly, however, the mass arched skyward and scattered. A shape erupted from the floor, a seven-headed, roaring shape; as it moved, Marie sprang backward; her arm hit the glass doors of the toy cabinet, which cracked, and the room swam before her eyes. When her vision cleared, she found herself among giants: She had shrunk, it seemed. Table legs soared into the air above her head; higher still—a distant mountain—rose the Christmas tree. All around, the beasts skittered and squealed—vulnerable mice no longer, but great, hairy, long-toothed creatures, terrifying to behold. And in their midst, their King loomed, screeching for plunder with his seven mouths.

The Mouse King's cry was answered by a shout from above. On the Christmas table, the Nutcracker stood, no longer grotesque, but a tall, young man, brave in gold braid; so beautiful was he that he caught Marie's untried heart at once. In his hand he held a bright sword high as he called out his commands. From the broken glass cabinet, a bugle sounded and a drum stuttered into life; from the floor by the table where the hussars stood came an answering shout. The toy soldiers were toys no longer. Leaping from perch and pedestal, they roared in their regiments down to the battlefield.

And while the drums rolled and the bugles called, the fight was joined. Under the seven-headed King's command, the great mice formed companies to meet the charge of cavalry. Chaos followed, for while the mice lacked firearms and had no horses, they matched the horses in weight; their claws were long and their white teeth sharp, and the wounds they dealt were terrible. Again and yet again, the soldiers of the Nutcracker fell back and regrouped, fighting in ever-smaller companies under his command.

He was always to the fore, wielding a

Brave and brilliant in battle, the Nutcracker de-
feated the King of the mouse army.
With the death of their King, the night creatures
fled. Marie's heart was won.

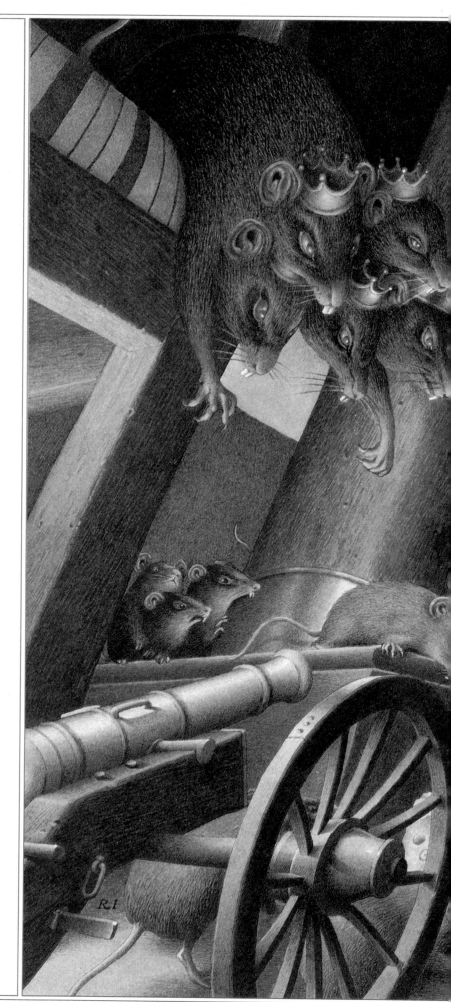

flashing blade, pressing through the throng toward the place where the Mouse King stood. The leaders met amid a welter of men and horses, of rearing mice, of bloodied corpses. It was impossible to see the fight of the pair; only the surge of the crowd told where they stood. But at the end, the ranks parted to show the Nutcracker stabbing and slashing at the Mouse King's throats. Blood spurted; the creature cried out with its multitude of voices and lunged forward. Marie, cowering at the edge of battle, enchanted by the valor of the hero and fearing for his life, gave a scream and crumpled; the last thing she saw before the darkness closed around her was Drosselmeier, perched on the clock like a demon of the air, his mouth stretched in a laugh she could not hear.

She awakened in sunlight, refracted through frost flowers that starred the parlor windowpane. Her face rested against the rough wool of the carpet. All around lay broken toy soldiers, stiffening mouse carcasses, shattered crockery and crumbled cakes and pastries. Amid the rubble were seven small golden crowns; Marie thought of the Mouse King's heads and closed her eyes again.

A thin, reedy voice—Drosselmeier's— called her name. Farther away, her mother spoke, and then Marie answered. The two of them bent over her and pried from her grasp the thing that she held: a soldier clothed in a hussar's uniform. Marie protested weakly, but her elders had her well in hand. She was carried to her bed. The doctor was sent for.

No one, it seemed, believed the tale Marie told. Her mother frowned and called it a dream, brought on by excitement and too many sweets. The doctor said the story was an imagining, caused by a brain fever that came from her fall against the glass cabinet.

Drosselmeier scoffed, too, when he was brought to the bedchamber. From the

Morning light fell on a scene of destruction: Marie unconscious, clutching the Nutcracker; the toys of Christmas lying broken among the scattered crowns of the King of the Mice.

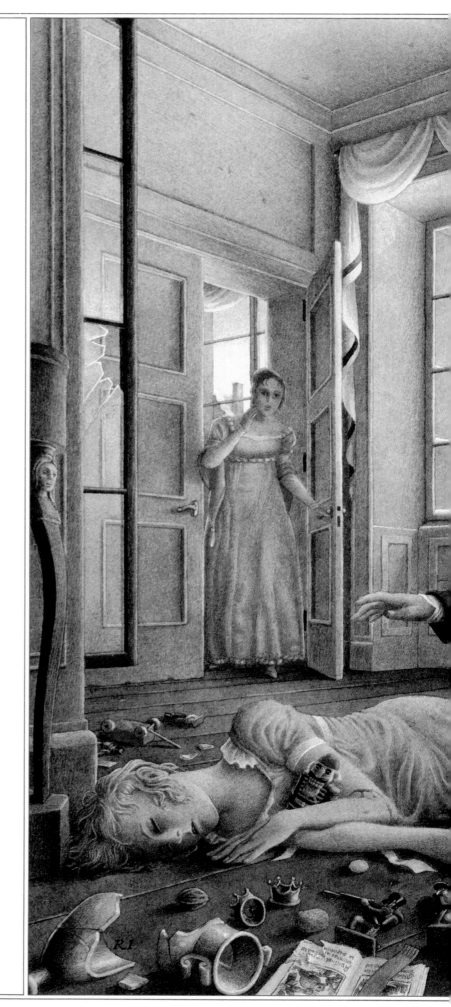

folds of his cloak, he withdrew the Nutcracker, a poor wooden thing in gaudy uniform, topped by a grotesque wooden head. Watching her with his bright eye, he presented the toy. "Here is your hero," he said. "Nothing but a block of wood, and an ugly one at that."

But Marie took the Nutcracker into her arms. "I love him nevertheless," she replied. "I owe him my life."

The clockmaker sighed. After a while he said, with every appearance of regret, "You are right. This creature is a prince of Faerie placed under an enchantment. The terms were that he slay the Mouse King and that a woman love him while he bore the form cast upon him. His world, you see, is full of dangers you cannot imagine. Will you then join him there?"

"I will join him."

"You leave behind forever your people and your home, and before you have reached the age to know your own world."

"I will join him," said Marie.

"You have had every chance to refuse," said Drosselmeier with a crooked smile.

And during the night of that day, the daughter of the Stahlbaum household disappeared. No one could tell where she had gone; no evidence of her was found by her parents. The storytellers said that she joined her prince in a land of milk and honey and reigned with him happily all her life long.

Drosselmeier, however, could have told a different tale. He went on about his eccentric business. He continued to make his wonderful toys and elaborate his enchanting castle. Sometimes he peered in the windows at its gallery, observing with satisfaction the dolls he had added to the company that paraded up and down. These were a handsome young man in a uniform, whose jacket was swagged with gold braid; he sat at the side of a pretty woman, hardly more than a girl, and the very image of Marie.

Because she gave her heart to the Nutcracker, a creature of the other world, Marie joined him in the castle of enchantment. There, like the Nutcracker, she danced to Drosselmeier's measure.

III

SUMMONING THE SUN

Once there was a King of Christmas. The French called him l'Abbé de la Malgouverné, or the Abbot of Misgovernment; to the Scots, he was the Abbot of Unreason. In some places in England, he was known as the King of the Bean; in others, as the Lord of Misrule. Sometimes he reigned from Allhallows Eve to Candlemas—October 31 to February 2—and thus presided over the whole of winter. Sometimes he oversaw the Twelve Days of Christmas only. He was the master of the Christmas revels, the author of pleasures for great households in the old days when England was merry.

He was often a rough fellow, chosen by lot to hold the holiday. In the old days, Christmas was a topsy-turvy time, a time to put on the mantle of another's nature: Servant became master, men donned women's garb, humans disguised themselves as animals, the better to enjoy the ease and gaiety that the season offered.

And indeed, Christmastide was a season of abundance and hilarity. The minstrels in their carved gallery high at one end of the hall of a great lord must have seen wonderful sights as they plucked their lutes and puffed at their pipes and sackbuts. In the hearth that loomed against one wall—a fireplace so large that three tall men could have lain in it head to foot—the Yule log blazed, casting its glow on oak paneling and stone walls decked with swags of holly and ivy. The fire shone on the master's high table, ranged along one end of the hall, and on the long trestle set at right angles to it. At the high table sat the Lord of Misrule, draped in ill-fitting velvet and fur and adorned with a tipsy hat; he was flanked by his fellow servants, who waited upon him with exaggerated care. At the other tables, the people of the household sat—men, women and children, arrayed in scarlet, in emerald, in canary yellow—laughing and shouting and singing. Maidservants laden with jugs of drink and great bowls of food moved up and down the rows of benches, nimbly avoiding pinches and tickles and the hounds at their feet.

From three in the afternoon until midnight on the first day of revelry, the noisy throng ate and drank. For each of the two courses, the minstrels blew a fanfare; then the warner—a miniature scene of hunting and jousting, molded from sugar and plaster—was ceremoniously borne through the great hall and set before the Lord of Misrule. It was the announcement of as many as twenty-five dishes—with such names as "mortrews" and "bucknade," "al-

lowes" and "hanoney"—that made up a course. Most of the food was stewlike, to ease the work of the guests, who used their spoons and fingers, not their forks, for eating. The dishes were made from the bounty of field, forest and stream—from fresh and salted venison, from pheasant, swan, capon, lamprey, crane, pike, heron, carp, kid, rabbit, mutton.

The diners tore at a peacock, boiled and reclothed in all its plumage; they spooned up frumenty—sweet grain porridge—and jellies shaped like castles, and blancmange, which was chicken pounded and boiled with rice, almond milk and honey. They dug at puddings made of dried plums, ale, sugar, suet and apples. For drink they had plenty: wines from Guienne, Anjou and Poitou, and good English ale. And best of all, they had the wassail bowl, brimming with hot ale, sugar and spices; apples floated 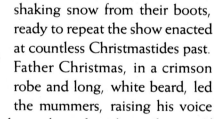 on surface foam so white and soft that the drink was sometimes called lamb's wool or old-man's-beard.

The very center of this feast, summoned by trumpet, greeted with carols and borne in a procession led by the Lord of Misrule himself, was the head of a boar. It lay on its charger, rimmed with red apples and nestled in a bed of rosemary and thyme, surveying the company with its prune eyes. Its jaw was muzzled with rush and willow; its tusks were made of almonds; and in its mouth was clenched a lemon, a delicacy brought from warmer lands.

While the contents of the head—spiced and pickled meat known as brawn—were distributed and the good food and ale passed from trencher to trencher and cup to cup, the Lord of Misrule called for games. For the elders there were dice games, played with dice of ivory and silver and bone; there were card games; there were riddles. As the adults concentrated on these diversions, their children played blindman's buff among the tables or, with nervous fingers, dipped for raisins floating in bowls of flaming brandy—a sport they called snapdragon.

It was not long before Snap the Dragon himself appeared, for the games were only a foretaste of the Christmas entertainments. At a sign from the Lord of Misrule, village mummers danced into the hall, shaking snow from their boots, ready to repeat the show enacted at countless Christmastides past. Father Christmas, in a crimson robe and long, white beard, led the mummers, raising his voice to make his prologue heard over the roar of his unruly audience: "Here come I, Father Christmas; welcome or welcome not. I hope Old Father Christmas will never be forgot." This summoned the characters of the mummers' ancient play: Captain Slasher, the Heathen, in his Turk's dress; England's patron saint, George, keeping his eyes lifted heavenward to suggest an unblemished character; Doctor Brown; a tatterdemalion dragon called Snap; and an assortment of entertainers wearing horse and donkey and dog masks.

To the accompaniment of cheers and rhymes and howls of laughter, the mummers danced and acted out the play everyone knew. With boasts and shouts, the

villain, Captain Slasher, challenged Saint George to a duel; the Christian knight was the winner, and the Turk fell dead. Then Father Christmas summoned the Doctor, who brought the Turk to life and repentance. The dragon battle followed, with the audience cheering loudly for Saint George. Again the Christian hero triumphed. Again the Doctor revived the victim. But as Saint George explained, the story said the dragon died, and die it must. He therefore dispatched the beast with a blow of his wooden sword. Snap rolled to the ground and expired with a groan and a muffled snort.

Then the mummers sang praises to their raucous audience, wishing their patrons health and wealth as they danced around the tables, waving their wooden swords, nodding their beasts' heads at the tired, squealing children, holding out their leather purses for the Christmas coins the parents gave and bowing their thanks for the bounty.

And when the troops had vanished into the snow and the children had been sent to sleep, the older members of the household danced, sometimes in processional lines, sometimes in great circles. To the twinkling notes of lutes and the brisk taps of little drums, they trod the measures of the stately pavan; of the courante, with its cheerful running steps; of the galliard and of the lavolta, wild and bounding. Sometimes they sang as they danced, one calling the stanzas, the rest chanting the refrain. They were caroling for Christmas.

At the very last, when the fires burned low, they sang the song that brought Christmas home and made it part of the lives they knew, for the song was a lullaby to the Christ Child. The women sang:

> *This poor youngling*
> *For whom we do sing*
> *By, by, lully lullay*

And the men replied:

> *Lully, lulla, thou little tiny child*
> *By, by, lully lullay*

Ever more softly, they repeated the homely melody that they had sung since their childhoods and that their parents and grandparents had sung before them, until at length their voices faded. Then revelers left for their bedchambers, and the hall was still and empty, except for the pages on their pallets and the Yule log, hissing and crackling on the hearth.

So the Twelve Days of Christmas began in Christian countries. Merriment prevailed, and noise and fire and light. Yet Christianity — the reason for the festival — had not shaped it. Few of the revelers, who were simply doing what their parents and grandparents had done, could have identified the ancient origins of their customs: The tracks that led from old rites to the midwinter feast were as crisscrossed and tangled as the footprints of animals in the snow. They stemmed from the wintry gloom of Scandinavia, where Odin presided over the sunless privations of the solstice; from Celtic and Saxon lands; from Italy and sunny Greece.

The extravagantly merry element of Christmas went back as far as human knowledge, to the dim past when kings were sacrificed to ensure the land's health. In time, substitutes for the kings were cho-

Under the eyes of the Lord of Misrule, old Christmas feasts rollicked and roared.
Minstrels played, jugglers juggled, tumblers tumbled, and hidden within their beast masks, troops
of mummers enacted their ancient plays to celebrate life and light.

Singing as they went, people took the bounty of Christmas
across the fields of winter: the boar, a relic of sacrifices long-forgotten, and the Yule
log, whose fire would summon the returning sun.

sen. Among the Babylonians, some nonentity from the lower orders was made a mock king for the season and permitted to enjoy all the powers and privileges of kingship for the week preceding his death. By the end of imperial Rome, blood sacrifice was no longer a necessity, but the overturning of rank, and the anarchy and hilarity that went with it, remained.

From December 17 to December 24, the Romans celebrated Saturnalia to see out the old year and ensure the health of the winter-sown crops. Saturn was the god of sowing and had reigned over an ancient golden age, said the Romans. In the time of his power, there had been no crime, no punishment, no laws or judges, no need for farming, because the earth produced without cultivation all that people needed: Milk and nectar flowed in the rivers, and honey dripped from the ilex tree. The old god had been deposed, but at the solstice, folk relived his happy reign. Recalling the days of his power, they closed schools, law courts and markets, suspended all military operations and did more or less whatever they wanted to do. A slave was chosen by lot to be King, and his word was law; in every household, his fellow slaves were turned into masters and the masters into slaves. Whatever nonsensical request the household sovereign made was granted. This Saturnalia King was the ancestor of the Lord of Misrule and the King of the Bean; the beans or coins or figures hidden in Christmas puddings and – in France – in Twelfthnight cakes recalled the old custom of choosing a seasonal King by lot.

The week of Saturnalia was known for feasting, for unbridled license and for disguising: To turn the world upside down, men dressed as women and clothed themselves in beast pelts and masks. And it was a time of gift-giving. People presented one another with *strenae* – boughs of laurel and evergreen for the bringing of luck; the name commemorates the woodland goddess Strenia, from whose sacred groves the branches came. Children received *sigillaria*, small dolls of clay that were sold at a special fair held during the season.

Because Saturnalia occurred at the solstice, it was a festival of lights. Chief among the presents people exchanged were candles that would burn throughout the winter nights, summoning the moribund sun back to life.

Feasting and nonsense, the giving of gifts, the lighting of lights, all were absorbed into the Christian Christmas celebration, fixed in the Fourth Century on December 25, so that it might displace the rituals of the great pagan winter festivals. The Roman legacy to Christianity was altogether jollier than the Yuletide activities of northern Europe, where the winter ritual was a feast of the dead, crowded with malign spirits and devils and with the haunting presence of Odin and his night riders. But even there, the nights were filled with feasting, with boisterous "drinking Yule," and with the elements that were a part of winter festivals everywhere: fire and light. The great midwinter fires of the Norsemen lived on in the Yule log that filled familial hearths.

The Yule log's sacred origins were revealed in the ceremonies and beliefs that clung to it, all of them associated with health and fecundity. In England, the log was cut and dragged home by oxen or horses, and the people sang as they walked beside it. Often it was decorated with evergreens and sometimes sprinkled with grain or with cider before it was set alight. In Yugoslavia, where the log was cut before dawn on Christmas Eve and carried into the house at twilight, the wood was adorned with flowers and silk and gold, then doused with an offering of wine and grain. Provençal families tripped out together to fetch their log, singing blessings on their women, crops and flocks as they did so. Their Yule log, called the *tréfoire*, was carried three times around the house and christened with wine before it was set afire.

Everywhere, the log was charged with beneficent magic. It was kept burning for twelve hours or for twelve days, warming hands and hearts, and when its fire was quenched, a fragment of the wood was saved to light the next year's log. The burning protected the household against witchcraft; the ashes were scattered over the fields to make them fertile, or cast into wells to purify the water, or used in various charms: to free cattle from vermin, to ward off hailstorms. In Germany, the remnants of the log were thought to protect a house against lightning.

In that Christmas fire blazed joy at the returning light; the log bore within itself the fires of spring. That was the brightness that all solstice celebrations, from Saturnalia to Yule, included and, as the years wore on, came to emphasize.

The same delight was to be seen in the mummers' plays of Christmas. The mummers, with their beast masks and their comical costumes, were the rag, tag and bobtail of long-forgotten rites—old sacrifices recalled with gaiety. The names of the characters changed from village to village and from decade to decade: Sometimes the host who introduced the show was Father Christmas—not a gift bringer but the soul of winter, serving as master of ceremonies. Sometimes the hero was Saint George, sometimes King William, sometimes King George. Some companies included a dragon, some a horse, but other characters might well appear—an ox, a goat, a dog, a deer. Whatever the cast and no matter how the verses changed as they were passed from generation to generation of mummers (or guisers, as they were also called), the plots remained essentially the same: A hero fought an enemy and slew him or was slain; then a doctor brought the dead to life again. So did the sun seem to die and revive; so did the world die in winter and live again each spring.

As the sun's crisis passed each year, the balance of magic tipped in favor of friendly forces. The tales told then were of good magic and of kind enchantments.

People gazed with affection at the animals around them, for instance. The beasts partook of the spell of Christmas. Everyone knew the tale of the moment of the Nativity, when time paused in its course. The animals of field and wood spoke then, said the storytellers, in Latin words that matched the sounds peculiar to their species:

Christus natus est (Christ is born), the cock crowed.

Quando? (When?) croaked the raven.

As winter deepened in the far north, the sun hid itself from human
view. Norsemen sent scouts to the high mountains to watch for the first streak of returning
light. When it was seen, the great Yule feasts began.

From town to town went Father Christmas with his mummers and their stage.
They enacted the Saint George play, in which the dead were brought to life, even as the dying
sun returned to shine again when the darkest winter day had passed.

Hac nocte (This night), the rook replied. *Ubi?* (Where?) lowed the ox.

The sheep said the place was Bethlehem, and the ass brayed *Eamus* (Let us go).

And most animals obeyed. The stork came swiftly, plucking its own feathers to soften the infant's bed, and so remained the patron of babies ever after. The robin fanned the fire in the cave of Bethlehem and kept it burning throughout the night. Its red breast—singed by the flames—was the mark of its generosity. The nightingale nested near the manger. It had never sung before that night, but the choirs of angels roused it. The bird caroled with them, and its heavenly song remained an echo of the glory. The cat appeared, but disdained to join the kneeling beasts and only mumbled in recognition; amused at its independence, Mary blessed it, saying that it would always live at man's hearth but never be man's servant. The owl did not rouse itself to join its fellows. It was condemned to perpetual penance, hiding by day, and by night crying mournfully, "Who will guide me to the newborn? Who? Who?"

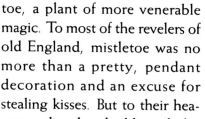

Each Christmas, the people said, the animals were free to speak once more. Whoever ventured to the stable would hear the deep whispers of the cattle; in the fold, the sheep muttered among themselves. In their hives, the bees sang canticles in perfect harmony.

They sang that the cloud of midwinter had lifted. Gale, frost, snow and ice would continue, but there was another climate invisible and impalpable, which brimmed with promise. On Christmas Eve, it was said, the trees of the forest, no matter how bare and black of branch, sprang into full flower, fruit and leaf—although few people ever saw that wonder.

Some fortunate souls were favored with the sight of fern seed at Christmas; it was thought to be visible only at the solstices. If a man or woman could obtain the seed, they acquired enviable powers. They could discern things hidden from others' eyes. They could do the work of thirty people. For one night, the devil had to do their bidding, and the seed protected them against the devil's powers. Fern seed could make a person invisible. It could reveal the whereabouts of buried treasure. That was a power it shared with mistletoe, a plant of more venerable magic. To most of the revelers of old England, mistletoe was no more than a pretty, pendant decoration and an excuse for stealing kisses. But to their heathen ancestors, the plant had been holy, a seemingly free-living cluster of dark green leaves and greenish white berries ensconced high in the branches of trees, fruiting in midwinter and evincing a lofty contempt for the earth on which all other plants depended. Its untethered position between ground and sky made it a link between humankind and the life-giving sun. The men and women who laughed and kissed beneath it, following the custom, were paying respect to the fertility magic of their ancestors. Churchmen knew this, and they refused to allow the plant within the walls of their churches.

Of all trees, perhaps the apple was most fraught with old enchantment, enshrining

the potency of nature. It was the tree of fairyland and paradise, a talisman for entering the other world. Its fruit outlived other fruits, lasting into the depths of winter. Its juice fermented into a liquor that transported the mind. It was food and cheer at a time when both were scarce. It told its own future: If the sky was clear and the sun shone through the bare branches of an apple tree on Christmas morning, there would be a rich crop.

The owners of orchards were well aware of the tree's power, and at Christmas, they made sure that it was roused from its dormancy. In Austria, maidens ceremoniously hugged the trees. Or, less amiably, they knocked on the trunks and ordered them awake. In England, countryfolk sang the wassail in their orchards and honored one tree with a libation of cider. The tree they chose for the ceremony was the most respected in the orchard, usually the oldest, certainly the most prolific. It was called the Apple Tree Man, and on it depended the fate of the whole orchard.

It was well known that the Apple Tree Man had a spirit of its own and could confer benefits other than a bountiful apple harvest. The people of the orchard lands of Somerset could illustrate its power with many tales. One told of a farmer who died, having willed all of his land to his younger son and nothing to the elder. The younger man was mean, vain, spoiled and greedy. Although custom obliged him to distribute the inheritance fairly, he gave nothing to his brother except a tiny plot with two trees on it, an old donkey, a feeble ox, and a tumble-down cottage, for which he exacted a stiff rent. The elder brother was a good husbandman. He took the animals out into the lanes so that they could feed on the wayside grass; he patched their stable to make it comfortable. He carefully tended the two apple trees, and at length, his animals and trees began to flourish.

Christmas Eve arrived. The younger brother appeared, demanding his rent, and demanding also to be summoned at midnight, for he had heard that treasure was buried on the land and he thought that the animals, when they awakened and spoke, would guide him to it. His brother nodded and set about his business, feeding the donkey and the ox and wassailing the Apple Tree Man. When he had poured the fragrant liquid over the branches and sung the wassailing song, a voice issued from the tree, a creaking, throaty voice alive with ancient laughter.

"Dig here," the apple tree said, and bent its branches to the earth at its root.

The man dug as he was told. He uncovered a wooden chest, heavy with gold.

"Hide it away. It is yours," said the voice from the tree. "Then summon your brother to the stable, as he bade you."

The younger brother arrived; on silent feet, he crept to the stable door. He laid his ear against it and found that indeed the animals were speaking.

"The greedy fool who listens at the door thinks I will tell him where treasure lies," said the donkey.

"The treasure is one thing he will never find," answered the ox with satisfaction. "We know that it was taken away long

since." In the tiny orchard, where the elder brother stood, the Apple Tree Man quivered with laughter, but said not a word more. The younger brother had to go without; the elder prospered.

Some of the magic of trees was brought into people's houses at Christmas time. The ancient Romans adorned their houses with fir branches at Saturnalia and at the Kalendae—the New Year's celebration that followed—for fir trees were spirits of fertility, being ever green and undying. From time immemorial, the people of Austria had cut cherry, pear or hawthorn branches and brought them into the warmth of their houses, and by keeping them in water or wet sand, they forced them to bloom for the Nativity.

From these customs, it seems, grew the tradition of the Christmas tree, glittering with lights, hung with fruit and with little gifts. But no one could say with certainty how the transformation was made. In Christian legend, a fir tree was the tree of life that grew in the Garden of Eden; when Eve plucked its fruit, its foliage and flowers shrank to needles. Only on the night of the Nativity did it bloom once more—a moment mirrored by the Christmas tree of the Christians.

Some chroniclers attributed the origin of the Christmas tree to Wilfred of Crediton, an Eighth Century Christian missionary who sought souls in pagan Germany. He felled an oak, sacred to Odin and used for human sacrifice. A small fir tree sprang up nearby, and this unstained plant, Wilfred declared, was the emblem of the new faith. Other scholars offered a different explanation. They said that the

great reformer Martin Luther was so enchanted with the splendor of the stars one Christmas Eve that he adorned a fir tree with candles to emulate their light and presented it to his children.

The first Christmas trees were described by an anonymous Frenchman fifty years after Luther's death. "At Christmas," he wrote, "they set up fir trees in the parlors at Strasbourg and hang thereon roses cut out of many-colored paper, apples, wafers, gold foil and sweets." In the following centuries, the custom spread across the Continent: Almost every house had a fir tree that defied December's bareness with its decorations of fruit and blossoms and blazing lights.

And what of the presents that hung upon the tree and appeared on Christmas Eve and Christmas morning? They were descendants, perhaps, of the *strenae* and *sigillaria* of the Roman Saturnalia, but they were more: They were part of the good will and good magic of the season of the returning sun.

Unlikely giftgivers came out of hiding then. Trolls, elves and goblins could be dangerous, since they were creatures of the other world, but many Christmas stories showed that, in their capricious way, they could be kind as well.

In Saxony, for instance, in a wood near the village of Kirscha, there stood until recent times a pillar commemorating an act of elfin generosity. That deed occurred on a bitterly cold Christmas Eve. Keen east winds had blown for days, and heavy snows had drifted over roads and paths, making it difficult for horses, let alone people, to walk. The fir trees of the

The julnissen

The Christmas gift bringers of Norway and Denmark were
household elves that lived during the year in attics and stables. On Christmas Eve, they emerged to hide presents all around the house.

Befana

An old woman who rode a broomstick through the air
gave Italian children presents at Christmas if they were good, coals if they
were not. Befana was her name; she journeyed on Epiphany Eve.

Christkindl

Riding a tiny deer laden with sweets and toys, an angel
visited German families every Christmas Eve. The pretty creature was an
emissary from heaven and so was called the Christ Child.

Kolyada

On Christmas Eve in Russia, a white-robed elf-maiden
traveled by sleigh from house to house. The children of the villages sang carols
to honor her; Kolyáda rewarded them with Christmas treats.

Saint Nicholas

Best-known and -loved of Christmas spirits was Saint Nick,
whose horse's hoofs were heard on Dutch rooftops on the eve of December 6. He
slid down chimneys, bringing things to fill the young ones' shoes.

Gifts sometimes came by winter magic and from unexpected quarters.
This happened to a poor man who chanced upon a dwarf's cave. He started back in fear, for dwarfs
could be dangerous. But the little creature had presents to give.

great wood stood dour and forbidding against the gray sky, their branches drooping under their white burden. Through this dismal scene trudged a middle-aged man, a day laborer seeking to collect the wages he was owed by a woman in the village. He was a poor man, the father of six children, and his name was Reini. The wages he sought meant food in the mouths of his children. The walk was ten miles, and disappointment greeted him at the end. The woman heard him without sympathy. Her husband was away, she said bluntly, and Reini would be paid when he came back.

Stolidly, Reini nodded. The door slammed behind him. He turned into the wind and began to retrace his footsteps.

After he had traveled a few miles into the lonely wood, he spied a light. He approached and found that it marked the mouth of a cave he had not seen before. A tiny figure stood at the entrance – a dwarf, or an elf. Reini backed away: He knew about elvish mischief, and his luck was bad enough already.

But the little creature beckoned and called out in its high, piping voice. Then Reini saw a marvel. The pine branches that decorated the entrance of the cave were hung with all kinds of delicacies and fruits: honey cakes and sugar candy, hazelnuts and almonds, sugar plums and tiny tarts, all glittering in the darkness. The elf was watching him, his wrinkled face creased by a broad smile.

"I know when a man needs a helping hand," he said. "Here is a sack. Fill it with good things to please your young ones." And when Reini had filled the sack, the elf waved his thanks away, saying the treasure cost him nothing.

At first, the load seemed light to the tired man. But as he plunged into the darkness, with owls hooting and shadows flitting among the tree trunks, the sack grew heavier. Still he stumbled on, the sack cutting into his shoulder and the wind hurling needles in his face.

He reached his cottage at last. When he released the sack from his cold-stiffened hands, the children gathered around, exclaiming. Out of the sack's dark mouth tumbled cakes and candies, fruit and nuts – and coins of dazzling gold. Old magic had brought the family the wherewithal to survive the winter.

The elf was one of a legion of enchanted giftgivers. Some, such as the *julnissen* and *jultomten* of Scandinavia, were elder hearth spirits who lived in dark corners or under stairs; on Christmas Eve, while their households were sleeping, they emerged from hiding to feast on the porridge that the children of the house had left for them and to hide Christmas packages in unexpected places. Some were descendants of old gods and goddesses: The crone Befana of Italy bore a name that derived from the word "Epiphany." And it was Epiphany Eve when Befana, like the hearth goddess Berchta, her ancestress, left trinkets for well-behaved young ones and coals for those who were naughty.

Of all the other-world creatures freed by the season, the best-known was Saint Nicholas, or Father Christmas or Santa Claus, patron of thousands of children, British and Dutch among them – a benign, puffing, elvish emanation of the season.

Linked in spirit to Scandinavia's legendary World Tree, to fir
boughs hung in Roman houses, and to branches brought indoors by Austrians to
flower in winter, a decorated tree became the sign of Christmas.

A Russian tale told how a couple shaped a maiden from the snows
of the cold season. She came to life and spent her days among mortals, but those days
were brief: The sun of springtime melted her to mist.

Never was a creature's identity so coiled and curlicued, so wreathed in different magics; he trailed a pedigree as tangled and matted as a kitten makes a ball of yarn. This genial provider owed part of his character to the Norse god Odin, who flew the winter skies, able to cure disease and tell the future. Some of Father Christmas' magic came from Melchior, oldest of the Three Kings who followed the star to Bethlehem, bringing gifts to the Christ Child. A pious and supremely generous Christian, Saint Nicholas added his name to this creature of grand affability.

Saint Nicholas and Christmas trees, feasting and merriment—these embodied what Christmas came to be: the triumph of light over the dark, the promise of riches in the impoverished season. So joyful was the celebration, so replete with human victory, that winter itself seemed weakened: not a venerable giant cruel in his cold power, but a vulnerable maiden, trembling in the hands of humankind.

Or so a Russian tale suggested. The story told of a woodcutter and his wife, childless and lonely, who one winter day fashioned a *snegurochka*—a maiden of snow—to amuse themselves. Delighted with their fair creation, they called her Daughter, and when they did so, enchantment happened. Dark eyes gleamed in the pale snow face, and rosy color brushed the frozen lips. The statue trembled to life, clothed not in snow and ice but in an ivory-colored velvet cap and robe, adorned with pearls and edged with white fur. The maiden held out her hand to the man and woman and smiled upon them.

Some storytellers said the Snow Maiden was a miracle, sent to comfort the couple in their old age; others declared that she was an ancient spirit, the daughter of spring and winter come to earth. Whatever her nature, she remained with the couple, pale and quiet, but as loving and dutiful as a true daughter would be. Then, as winter waned and people began to leave their houses, the Snow Maiden fell in love with a young man of the woodcutter's village, thus surrendering her heart to humankind and acquiring the mortality that was the human lot.

Her death came quietly, on a day when she walked with her lover through a birch wood. The trees were still bare in the wood, but the ice that coated their branches dripped down in ribbons, glittering in the sun of early spring. The ground beneath the trees was a patchwork of white snow and brown earth. Green shoots pushed up in the places where the snow had retreated. The youth played his flute; the Snow Maiden walked beside him, turning her face to the sunlight. At length, she gave the faintest sigh and seemed to dwindle. Then nothing was left but an icy mist, drifting upward into the blue sky. The frail winter creature could not survive the breath of spring.

It was always so, and everyone knew it: Winter would give way to light and life. Where the snow had lain, snowdrops and daffodils would appear; the dull fields would shine with the early wheat; and in the pastures, lambs would play. Knowing this, people laughed in the heart of winter; they sang for the radiance of the Christ Child, and they sang for themselves, who would live to see another spring.

The Songs of Christmas

To celebrate Christmas, the whole universe sang, it seemed. In the heavens, the stars and planets danced majestic rounds, forming patterns shaped by harmonies inaudible to human ears. Below, the churches and cathedrals echoed with the hymns of the Nativity as choirs sent their good tidings soaring skyward. In field and forest, birds offered their musical praises. And in village lane and castle courtyard, in hall and hovel, the people caroled.

The carolers' gaiety was a terrestrial reflection of the celestial movement of the spheres: The first carols were round dances, in which leaders sang the stanzas and followers chanted the refrains. But the singers' purpose was not so grand. They sang of themselves. Sometimes their verses embodied ancient, half-forgotten beliefs: that bringing live evergreens into a house protected it against the scourge of winter; that the words of the wassail—in Anglo-Saxon *wes hāl*, or "good health"—could endow people and animals alike with well-being; that holly, the plant of men, warred always with clinging ivy, the women's vine. Sometimes the songs cast the Nativity in homely terms, telling tales of how all nature served the Christ Child, how bird and beast, each in its fashion, made gifts for him, and how the great saints were permitted miracles in the heart of winter, when darkness was graced by the return of the light.

Deck the Hall with Boughs of Holly

Deck the hall with boughs of holly,
Fa la la la la, la la la la.
'Tis the season to be jolly,
Fa la la la la, la la la la.
Don we now our gay apparel,
Fa-la la-la la la la.
Troll the ancient Yuletide carol,
Fa la la la la, la la la la.

See the blazing Yule before us,
Fa la la la la, la la la la.
Strike the harp and join the chorus,
Fa la la la la, la la la la.
Follow me in merry measure,
Fa-la la-la la la la.
While I tell of Yuletide treasure,
Fa la la la la, la la la la.

Fast away the old year passes,
Fa la la la la, la la la la.
Hail the new, ye lads and lasses,
Fa la la la la, la la la la.
Sing we joyous all together,
Fa-la la-la la la la.
Heedless of the wind and weather,
Fa la la la la, la la la la.

Gloucestershire Wassail

Wassail, wassail, all over the town!
Our toast it is white, and our ale it is brown,
Our bowl it is made of the white maple tree;
With the wassailing bowl we'll drink to thee.

So here is to Cherry and to his right cheek,
Pray God send our master a good piece of beef,
And a good piece of beef that may we all see;
With the wassailing bowl we'll drink to thee.

And here is to Dobbin and to his right eye,
Pray God send our master a good Christmas pie,
And a good Christmas pie that may we all see;
With our wassailing bowl we'll drink to thee.

So here is to Broad May and to her broad horn,
May God send our master a good crop of corn,
And a good crop of corn that may we all see;
With the wassailing bowl we'll drink to thee.

And here is to Fillpail and to her left ear,
Pray God send our master a happy New Year,
And a happy New Year as e'er he did see;
With our wassailing bowl we'll drink to thee.

And here is to Colly and to her long tail,
Pray God send our master he never may fail
A bowl of strong beer; I pray you draw near,
And our jolly wassail it's then you shall hear.

Come, butler, come fill us a bowl of the best,
Then we hope that your soul in heaven may rest;
But if you do draw us a bowl of the small,
Then down shall go butler, bowl and all.

Then here's to the maid in the lily white smock,
Who tripped to the door and slipped back the lock!
Who tripped to the door and pulled back the pin,
For to let these jolly wassailers in.

Holly and Ivy

Nay, ivy, nay, it shall not be I wis;
Let holly have the mastery, as the manner is.

Holly stands in the hall, fair to behold:
Ivy stands without the door, she is full sore a cold.
Nay, ivy, nay, it shall not be I wis;
Let holly have the mastery, as the manner is.

Holly and his merry men, they dance and they sing,
Ivy and her maidens, they weep and they wring.
Nay, ivy, nay, it shall not be I wis;
Let holly have the mastery, as the manner is.

Ivy hath chapped fingers, she caught them from the cold,
So might they all have, aye, that with ivy hold.
Nay, ivy, nay, it shall not be I wis;
Let holly have the mastery, as the manner is.

Holly hath berries as red as any rose,
The forester, the hunter, keep them from the does.
Nay, ivy, nay, it shall not be I wis;
Let holly have the mastery, as the manner is.

Ivy hath berries as black as any sloe;
There come the owl and eat him as she go.
Nay, ivy, nay, it shall not be I wis;
Let holly have the mastery, as the manner is.

Holly hath birds a fair full flock,
The nightingale, the popinjay, the gentle laverock.
Nay, ivy, nay, it shall not be I wis;
Let holly have the mastery, as the manner is.

Good ivy, what birds hast thou?
None but the owlet that cries how, how.
Nay, ivy, nay, it shall not be I wis;
Let holly have the mastery, as the manner is.

Stefan Was a Stable Boy

Stefan was a stable boy,
We thank him now tonight.
He waters his good horses five
To follow star so bright.
Through the night so dark and cold,
All the stars kept twinkling, shining bright.

Red were two of Stefan's horses,
Riding out so sprightly;
They knew that they must follow now
The star that shone so brightly.
Of five horses, two were white
That went riding out that starry night.

Of five horses, one was gray,
That one did Stefan ride;
He carried Stefan all the way,
He was good Stefan's guide.
Stefan rode the dapple-gray
All that long, dark, cold and wintry way.

Stefan rode and traveled far
With horses five that night;
He rode and came to Bethlehem,
Where shone the star so bright.
There in stable lay the Child,
Born of virgin maid so sweet and mild.

Stefan left then Bethlehem,
To Herod he went riding;
To tell the King a child was born
Who would be King of all men.
Herod then in anger flew,
Raged and stormed and said it was not true.

"If this roasted cock will crow
Three times, then I'll believe you."
He said, "Old rooster, rise and crow,
Oh, crow if this be true."
And that rooster on the plate
Rose and crowed as rooster crows at daybreak!

Drink to Stefan this good Yule,
Oh, drink a Stefan-cup;
To joy and love for all good men,
To rooster too who rose up,
And to horses five who went
Following the star with good Saint Stefan.

I Saw Three Ships

I saw three ships come sailing in,
On Christmas Day, on Christmas Day;
I saw three ships come sailing in,
On Christmas Day in the morning.

And what was in those ships all three,
On Christmas Day, on Christmas Day?
And what was in those ships all three,
On Christmas Day in the morning?

Our Savior Christ and his lady,
On Christmas Day, on Christmas Day;
Our Savior Christ and his lady,
On Christmas Day in the morning.

Pray whither sailed those ships all three,
On Christmas Day, on Christmas Day?
Pray whither sailed those ships all three,
On Christmas Day in the morning?

Oh, they sailed into Bethlehem,
On Christmas Day, on Christmas Day;
Oh, they sailed into Bethlehem,
On Christmas Day in the morning.

And all the bells on earth shall ring,
On Christmas Day, on Christmas Day;
And all the bells on earth shall ring,
On Christmas Day in the morning.

And all the angels in heaven shall sing,
On Christmas Day, on Christmas Day;
And all the angels in heaven shall sing,
On Christmas Day in the morning.

And all the souls on earth shall sing,
On Christmas Day, on Christmas Day;
And all the souls on earth shall sing,
On Christmas Day in the morning.

Then let us all rejoice amain,
On Christmas Day, on Christmas Day;
Then let us all rejoice amain,
On Christmas Day in the morning.

115

The Stork

The Stork she rose on Christmas Eve
And said unto her brood,
I now must fare to Bethlehem
To view the Son of God.

She gave to each his dole of meat,
She stowed them fairly in,
And fair she flew and fast she flew,
And came to Bethlehem.

Now where is He of David's line?
She asked at house and hall,
He is not here, they spake hardly,
But in the manger stall.

She found Him in the manger stall
With that most holy maid;
The gentle Stork she wept to see
The Lord so rudely laid.

Then from her panting breast she plucked
The feathers white and warm;
She strewed them in the manger bed
To keep the Lord from harm.

Now blessed be the gentle Stork
Forever more quoth He,
For that she saw my sad estate,
And showed pity.

Full welcome shall she ever be
In hamlet and in hall,
And called henceforth the Blessed Bird
And friend of babies all.

The Friendly Beasts

Jesus, our brother, kind and good,
Was humbly born in a stable rude.
The friendly beasts around Him stood,
Jesus, our brother, kind and good.

"I," said the donkey, all shaggy and brown.
"I carried His mother uphill and down,
I carried her safely to Bethle'm town."
"I," said the donkey, all shaggy and brown.

"I," said the cow, all white and red.
"I gave Him my manger for a bed,
I gave Him my hay to pillow His head."
"I," said the cow, all white and red.

"I," said the sheep with the curly horn.
"I gave Him my wool for a blanket warm,
He wore my coat on Christmas morn."
"I," said the sheep with the curly horn.

"I," said the dove from the rafters high.
"I cooed Him to sleep so He would not cry,
We cooed Him to sleep, my mate and I."
"I," said the dove from the rafters high.

So every beast, by some good spell,
In the stable rude was glad to tell
Of the gift he gave Immanuel,
The gift he gave Immanuel.

Carol of the Birds

From out of a wood a cuckoo did fly,
  Cuckoo,
He came to a manger with joyful cry,
  Cuckoo;
He hopped, he curtsied, round he flew,
And loud his jubilation grew,
  Cuckoo, cuckoo, cuckoo.

A pigeon flew over to Galilee,
  Vrercoo,
He strutted, and cooed, and was full of glee,
  Vrercoo;
And showed with jeweled wings unfurled,
His joy that Christ was in the world,
  Vrercoo, vrercoo, vrercoo.

A dove settled down upon Nazareth,
  Tsucroo,
And tenderly chanted with all his breath,
  Tsucroo;
"O you," he cooed, "so good and true,
My beauty do I give to you —
  Tsucroo, tsucroo, tsucroo."

Good King Wenceslas

Good King Wenceslas looked out
On the Feast of Stephen,
When the snow lay round about,
Deep and crisp and even.
Brightly shone the moon that night,
Though the frost was cruel,
When a poor man came in sight,
Gathering winter fuel.

"Hither, page, and stand by me,
If thou know'st it telling,
Yonder peasant, who is he?
Where and what his dwelling?"
"Sire, he lives a good league hence,
Underneath the mountain;
Right against the forest fence,
By Saint Agnes' fountain."

"Bring me flesh, and bring me wine,
Bring me pine logs hither;
Thou and I will see him dine,
When we bear them thither."
Page and monarch forth they went,
Forth they went together;
Through the rude wind's wild lament,
And the bitter weather.

"Sire, the night is darker now,
And the wind blows stronger;
Fails my heart, I know not how,
I can go no longer."
"Mark my footsteps, good my page!
Tread thou in them boldly;
Thou shalt find the winter's rage
Freeze thy blood less coldly."

In his master's steps he trod,
Where the snow lay dinted;
Heat was in the very sod
Which the saint had printed.
Therefore, Christian men, be sure,
Wealth or rank possessing,
Ye who now will bless the poor,
Shall yourselves find blessing.

The Twelve Days of Christmas

On the first day of Christmas
   my true love sent to me
a partridge in a pear tree.

On the second day of Christmas
   my true love sent to me
two turtle doves,
and a partridge in a pear tree.

On the third day of Christmas
   my true love sent to me
three French hens,
two turtle doves,
and a partridge in a pear tree.

On the fourth day of Christmas
   my true love sent to me
four calling birds,
three French hens,
two turtle doves,
and a partridge in a pear tree.

On the fifth day of Christmas
   my true love sent to me
five gold rings,
four calling birds,
three French hens,
two turtle doves,
and a partridge in a pear tree.

On the sixth day of Christmas
   my true love sent to me
six geese a-laying,
five gold rings,
four calling birds,
three French hens,
two turtle doves,
and a partridge in a pear tree.

On the seventh day of Christmas
   my true love sent to me
seven swans a-swimming,
six geese a-laying,
five gold rings,
four calling birds,
three French hens,
two turtle doves,
and a partridge in a pear tree.

On the eighth day of Christmas
   my true love sent to me
eight maids a-milking,
seven swans a-swimming,
six geese a-laying,

125

five gold rings,
four calling birds,
three French hens,
two turtle doves,
and a partridge in a pear tree.

On the ninth day of Christmas
    my true love sent to me
nine ladies dancing,
eight maids a-milking,
seven swans a-swimming,
six geese a-laying,
five gold rings,
four calling birds,
three French hens,
two turtle doves,
and a partridge in a pear tree.

On the tenth day of Christmas
    my true love sent to me
ten lords a-leaping,
nine ladies dancing,
eight maids a-milking,
seven swans a-swimming,
six geese a-laying,
five gold rings,
four calling birds,
three French hens,
two turtle doves,
and a partridge in a pear tree.

On the eleventh day of Christmas
    my true love sent to me
eleven pipers piping,
ten lords a-leaping,
nine ladies dancing,
eight maids a-milking,
seven swans a-swimming,
six geese a-laying,
five gold rings,
four calling birds,
three French hens,
two turtle doves,
and a partridge in a pear tree.

On the twelfth day of Christmas
    my true love sent to me
twelve drummers drumming,
eleven pipers piping,
ten lords a-leaping,
nine ladies dancing,
eight maids a-milking,
seven swans a-swimming,
six geese a-laying,
five gold rings,
four calling birds,
three French hens,
two turtle doves,
and a partridge in a pear tree.

THE LIGHT TRIUMPHANT

"Glory to God in the highest, and on earth, peace, good will toward men." So the angels in their starry choir sang in the midnight sky above Bethlehem, heralding the newborn King to shepherds in the fields below. And when the celestial harmonies faded, when the great star rose and hung lamplike in the heavens, unutterably beautiful, magically near, the men were freed from their enchantment. Slowly they rose; they took up their staffs and, without a word, set their feet on the rocky track that led across the hills to Bethlehem.

All around them, the world was waking. Generations of believers would tell how fragrance floated on the air: The balsam gardens of En-gedi, on the shore of the Dead Sea, broke into full bloom at the moment of the Nativity, wrapping Bethlehem in their scent. At the shepherds' feet, the tiny, starlike rose of Jericho unfurled its petals, having sprung from a footprint left by Mary. It would bloom ever after, the storytellers said. By the roadside, a rosemary bush flowered blue, not white as it always had before. It had been brushed by the Virgin's blue cloak.

Thus, Christians lovingly shaped the story and told how all nature and all hu-mankind bowed to the Infant Jesus at His birth. Of the wise men who came to pay homage, for instance, the chronicler Matthew wrote only that, guided by the star, they journeyed from the east to Jerusalem; they inquired of Herod the King where they might find the Child, and Herod sent them to Bethlehem, charging them to return with news of the Infant. Herod had no wish to nurture a child called the King of the Jews. The wise men traveled on, following the star, until they found the center of their joy. They fell down and worshipped Jesus and brought Him treasures—gold and frankincense and myrrh. Then, wrote Matthew, "being warned of God in a dream that they should not return to Herod, they departed into their own country another way."

It was a simple story as told by Matthew. The Christians of later eras made it rich and strange. The star that appeared at Jesus' birth, they said, was recognized far away, on a mountain summit in India, as a sign long looked for. It was a star unlike any other, unfixed in course, floating freely in the firmament; some said the image of the Virgin shone in it, with a radiant, crowned Infant in her arms.

The Indian mountain was called Fons by some, Victorialis by others. Legend said that it was the tallest mountain in In-

dia, yet its summit was broad and flat, dotted with trees, glades, springs and grottoes. For those who watched the heavens from this lofty vantage, no hardship lay in living in the cool air.

But who the watchers were was a matter of dispute. Some accounts made them descendants of Balaam, an ancient, sinful seer described in the Old Testament Book of Exodus. Balaam, in the days of Israel's wanderings, had foretold the appearance of a star whose uncanny brightness would herald the world's rebirth. He, the story ran, had directed his sons to the mountain to pass their days looking for the star's appearance, and the vigil was handed down through the generations.

Other accounts said that the wise men came from the stock of Shem, Ham and Japhet, Noah's sons. Or that they were the twelve wisest astronomers of Chaldea and Persia, sent by the potentates of those empires. But most versions of the story made them kings. They had traveled to the mountain on the advice of their soothsayers and kept watch for the star from different parts of the plateau. The eldest of them was Melchior, King of Arabia. He was sixty. The youngest, Gaspar, was twenty. He ruled over Tharsis. Balthasar, King of Sheba, was forty.

In addition to the sight of the star, each of them received a special sign of the Savior's arrival. At that hour, an ostrich kept by Gaspar hatched two eggs, one yielding a lion, the other a lamb. A bird flew from a tall cedar in Melchior's garden and announced the birth of Jesus in a human voice. To Balthasar was born a son with the power of speech fully developed; the child told that Jesus' mother would be a virgin and that He would live for thirty-three years, while Balthasar's son himself would survive only thirty-three days.

So the Kings set off without delay; they had long been ready. Clad in silks and cloth of gold, leading trains of slaves carrying provisions and gifts, they journeyed toward Bethlehem. Across lonely desert and windy mountain they rode, guided always by the wonderful star, until they reached Jerusalem and King Herod, and spoke with him, and left him.

The star vanished. But the Three Kings rode steadily west and presently climbed the hill to Bethlehem. There they paused at a well. On the surface of the water, their own images shone, and behind them was reflected the evening sky. In it, clear and bright, the star swam. They had come to the place they had sought.

At the heart of the cave beneath the hill, the luminous manger stood, enfolding Joseph and Mary in its light. The crude cradle was lined with herbs and flowers – clover, wild thyme and the *Galium verum*, or Our-Lady's-bedstraw, that grows in British hedgerows. The holy hay, or sainfoin, lay there too, and of its own accord, it rose and curled to make a wreath for the Infant's head. All around the manger were ranged the beasts of farm and field: ox and ass and sheep and dog. Above the Child, a wren sang, safe in its nest in a niche in the rock.

Humble folk clustered at the cave entrance with their gifts. A shepherd held a lamb; another had a pair of doves; another laid his pipe by the Infant's side, in this fashion offering the music of the pastures.

At the edge of the cave, so children lat-

For those lacking gifts to give the Christ Child at the Nativity, miracles
occurred. To ease the heart of the maiden Madelon, who arrived empty-handed, the archangel
Gabriel struck the ground and caused the Christmas rose to bloom.

"Now when Jesus was born in Bethlehem of Judaea in the days of Her

e King, behold, there came wise men from the east to Jerusalem."

er said, a girl named Madelon huddled, weeping: She had come to worship but had no gift to give. A flash of light illumined her small form, as if a star had fallen at her feet. An angel stood by Madelon. He struck the hard ground with his staff, and flowers sprang up, white-petaled, with golden hearts. The girl Madelon plucked the blossoms and crept into the cave with them. Her gift was the Christmas rose.

Through the crowd strode the Three Kings. They were gentiles, come to bring the world's honor to the King of the Jews. Stiff in gold and silk, they walked among the people, and they kneeled as the people kneeled. Their offerings signified both joy and sorrow. Old Melchior brought thirty gold coins and a golden apple, treasures to crown the little King. Balthasar's gift was frankincense, a token of divinity. Gaspar's was bitter myrrh, the unguent used in embalming and thus a sign of the death the Child would die and the cold tomb that would briefly hold Him.

Then, with the shepherds' pipes singing and the children following until they reached the desert track that led away from Israel, the Three Kings departed, to bear witness in their own countries. It took them two years to reach their kingdoms and give the word to their people. Each of them lived to a very old age; before each King died, the star that had led them on their momentous pilgrimage appeared again for a brief span. In a later age, their remains were taken to Constantinople, then by ship to Milan and, long afterward, to the Cologne Cathedral, where they still lie behind the altar, encased in gold.

As time wore on, the tale of the Three Kings' journey was further embellished and their route extended. Simple folk said that they passed through Italy and asked guidance of the old woman Befana, who was too busy to greet or assist them. As punishment for her neglect, she had to wander the country each Christmas thereafter, searching for the Christ Child's countenance among the faces of the children. And it was said that every year for centuries after their burial, the Three Kings lived again on Epiphany Eve, riding through Spain to find the straw and the children's shoes that had been placed on window sills and balconies. The Kings' mounts fed on the straw; in gratitude, the men filled the shoes with gifts.

It was not that Spanish and Italian children believed that Italy and Spain lay between India and Bethlehem. Rather, all the activities surrounding the Nativity gradually were made part of everyday life. Men and women fitted the characters of the story into the scenes they knew best, imperceptibly melding the Christian tale with their own experience and with their old and cherished beliefs. So in the Hebrides, the Nativity was given a familiar setting, and the islanders themselves participated in the drama. In their telling of the story, Mary was seen sitting among the coastal rocks, knitting the Infant Jesus' clothes from the wool of Hebridean sheep. On the island of Eriskay, it was said, the village women gave her the wool. Later, they themselves had need; having no wool to give in return, the Virgin cut a long lock from the left side of her head and offered

that, the finest and softest of threads. Ever after, in memory of the gesture, the women of the island wore their hair thick on the right side and thin on the left.

As customs showed, the Nativity characters were vivid and immanent. The Christmas tables of Poland set a place for the Christ Child and a cushion of straw at the place, so that He might have a bed. German children's presents come from the Child or an angel representing Him.

To bring the glorious moment into home and heart, people made Christmas tableaux for all to gaze on in the winter season. These crèches—wrought by skilled hands from plaster, wood, satin, silk, paint and gilt—were portraits of their own lives as well as of the Nativity. The crèches of Naples, for instance, were wonderfully lifelike worlds in miniature. Mary, Joseph and Jesus were the center of the scene, to be sure. Over them  flew angels and cherubs, their bright robes frozen in sculptured folds. The Three Kings stood close, attended by turbaned servants who were adorned in pearls and gold and bore tasseled parasols. And clustered by these statues were the Neapolitans, caught in the midst of song or laughter or prayer. They, too, brought gifts for the Child. Court ladies, gowned in damask, lingered there; a woman in kerchief, shawl and apron spun wool; the butcher stood with his sides of beef, his hares, his braces of game; boys in knee breeches and embroidered waistcoats offered the fruits of the countryside: artichokes and cabbages, turnips, eggplants, melons.

Sometimes the tableaux were living enactments of the scene at Bethlehem. In churches and cathedrals all over Europe, children clothed as shepherds, as the Madonna, as the Magi, walked in procession toward the altar after the solemnities of the Christmas Eve Mass had ended, and donkeys and lambs walked with them. In front of the chancel, the players arranged themselves in joyful portrayal of the Savior's birth. The innocence of children and animals made the moment real once again.

The Christian story was the radiant heart of the season. Yet the branches garlanding churches and houses were the holly and ivy of elder beliefs; the customs surrounding the holiday were those of remote ages. Thus grim Odin, blended with generous Saint Nicholas and perhaps with the royal figure of Melchior, survives in the bluff and rubicund gift bringer, Santa Claus. Thus something of Yggdrasil—the World Tree of ancient Norsemen—lingers in the Christmas tree. Thus the old pagan sacrifices of winter were bent and shaped to new scenes, emerging as the mock heroics of Saint George in the mummers' plays or as village rites such as the hunting of the wren.

There was room for all of them in the new order, room for the elder gods and their ceremonies, room for the ancient ghosts of death and night, room for the lords of frost and snow. These memories were fitted by the common folk into the patterns of their lives and cherished without fear. In the Child born at Bethlehem, they had the promise of spring in the heart of midwinter, the divine gift of a bright, cleansing flame to drive away the dark.

"And when they were come into the house, they saw the young child with Mary his mother, and fell down, and worshipped him. And when they had opened their treasures, they presented unto him gifts."

Acknowledgments

The editors wish to express their gratitude to the following people and institutions for their assistance in the preparation of this volume: François Avril, Curator, Département des Manuscrits, Bibliothèque Nationale, Paris; Lydia Bayer, Spielzeugmuseum der Stadt Nürnberg, Nuremberg; Clark Evans, Rare Book and Special Collections Division, Library of Congress, Washington, D.C.; Marielise Göpel, Archiv für Kunst und Geschichte, West Berlin; Richard Gordon, British School at Rome, Italy; Bo Grandien, Docent i Konst Historia, Uppsala Universitet, Uppsala, Sweden; Dieter Hennig, Director, Brüder-Grimm-Museum, Kassel, Germany; Heidi Klein, Bildarchiv Preussischer Kulturbesitz, West Berlin; Rudolf Klemig, Director, Bildarchiv Preussischer Kulturbesitz, West Berlin; Gabrielle Kohler-Gallei, Archiv für Kunst und Geschichte, West Berlin; Ursula Lange-Lieberknecht, Brüder-Grimm-Museum, Kassel, Germany; Hartwig Lohse, Director, Universitätsbibliothek, Bonn; Justin Schiller, New York City; Robert Shields, Rare Book and Special Collections Division, Library of Congress, Washington, D.C.; Count Andrzej von Staufer, Cardiff, Wales; Rüdiger Vossen, Museum für Volkskunde, Hamburg; Ingeborg Weber-Kellermann, Marburg, Germany; Leonie von Wilkins, Germanisches Nationalmuseum, Nuremberg.

Bibliography

Auld, William Muir, *Christmas Traditions*. Detroit: Gale Research Company, 1968 (reprint of 1931 edition).*

Baker, Margaret, *Christmas Customs and Folklore*. Tring, England: Shire Publications, 1968.

Banks, Mary MacLeod, *British Calendar Customs*. Vols. 2 and 3. London: William Glaisher for The Folk-Lore Society, 1939.

The Bible: Designed to Be Read as Living Literature, the Old and the New Testaments in the King James Version. Ed. by Ernest Sutherland Bates. New York: Simon and Schuster, 1936.

The Book of Christmas. Pleasantville, New York: The Reader's Digest Association, 1973.*

Briggs, Katharine M.:
A Dictionary of British Folk-Tales in the English Language. London: Routledge & Kegan Paul, 1970.
An Encyclopedia of Fairies: Hobgoblins, Brownies, Bogies, and Other Supernatural Creatures. New York: Pantheon Books, 1976.

Bringsværd, Tor Åge, *Phantoms and Fairies from Norwegian Folklore*. Transl. by Pat Shaw Iversen. Oslo: Johan Grundt Tanum Forlag, no date.

Cagner, Ewert, comp., *Swedish Christmas*. Transl. by Yvonne Aboav-Elmquist. Gothenburg, Sweden: Tre Tryckare, 1954.

Campbell, R. J., *The Story of Christmas*. New York: The Macmillan Company, 1934.*

Cavendish, Richard, ed., *Man, Myth & Magic*. 11 vols. New York: Marshall Cavendish, 1983.

Chambers, E. K., *The Mediaeval Stage*. Vols. 1 and 2. London: Oxford University Press, 1948 (reprint of 1903 edition).

Chambers, R., ed., *The Book of Days: A Miscellany of Popular Antiquities in Connection with the Calendar*. 2 vols. Edinburgh, Scotland: W. & R. Chambers, 1863.

Coffin, Tristram Potter, *The Book of Christmas Folklore*. New York: The Seabury Press, 1973.

Cooke, Gillian, ed., *A Celebration of Christmas*. New York: G. P. Putnam's Sons, 1980.

Count, Earl W., *4000 Years of Christmas*. New York: Henry Schuman, 1948.*

Cowper, B. Harris, transl., *The Apocryphal Gospels and Other Documents Relating to the History of Christ*. 6th ed. London: David Nutt, 1897.

Craveri, Marcello, *The Life of Jesus*. Transl. by Charles Lam Markmann. New York: Grove Press, 1967.

Crippen, T. G., *Christmas and Christmas Lore*. Detroit: Gale Research Company, 1971.*

Croft, Aloysius, ed., *The Mystery of Christmas*. Milwaukee, Wisconsin: The Bruce Publishing Company, 1956.

Dawson, W. F., *Christmas: Its Origin and Associations, Together with Its Historical Events and Festive Celebrations during Nineteen Centuries*. Detroit: Gale Research Company, 1968 (reprint of 1902 edition).*

Dearmer, Percy, R. Vaughan Williams and Martin Shaw, *The Oxford Book of Carols*. London: Humphrey Milford for Oxford University Press, 1928.

Ditchfield, P. H., *Old English Customs Extant at the Present Time*. Detroit: Singing Tree Press, 1968 (reprint).*

Duncan, Edmondstoune, *The Story of the Carol* (The Music Story series). Detroit: Singing Tree Press, 1968 (reprint of 1911 edition).

Ebon, Martin, *Saint Nicholas: Life and Legend*. New York: Harper & Row, 1975.

Edersheim, Alfred, *Jesus the Messiah.* New York: Anson D. F. Randolph and Company, 1890.

The Editors of LIFE, *The Life Book of Christmas:*
Vol. 1, *The Glory of Christmas.* New York: Time Incorporated, 1963.
Vol. 2, *The Pageantry of Christmas.* New York: Time Incorporated, 1963.

Ehret, Walter, and George K. Evans, *The International Book of Christmas Carols.* Englewood Cliffs, New Jersey: Prentice-Hall, 1963.

Foley, Daniel J.:
The Christmas Tree: An Evergreen Garland Filled with History, Folklore, Symbolism, Traditions, Legends and Stories. Philadelphia: Chilton Company, 1960.
Christmas the World Over: How the Season of Joy and Good Will Is Observed and Enjoyed by Peoples Here and Everywhere. Philadelphia: Chilton Company, 1963.

Folkard, Richard, Jr., *Plant-Lore, Legends, and Lyrics.* London: Sampson Low, Marston, Searle, and Rivington, 1884.

Frazer, James George, *The New Golden Bough.* Ed. by Theodor H. Gaster. New York: New American Library, 1964.

Gallant, Roy A., *The Constellations: How They Came to Be.* New York: Four Winds Press, 1979.

Gaster, Theodor H., *New Year: Its History, Customs and Superstitions.* New York: Abelard-Schuman, 1955.*

Greene, Richard Leighton, ed., *The Early English Carols.* Oxford, England: Oxford University Press, 1977.

Grimm, Jacob, *Teutonic Mythology.* Transl. by James Steven Stallybrass. Vols. 1 and 3. Gloucester, Massachusetts: Peter Smith, 1976 (reprint of 1883 edition).

Grimm, Jakob Ludwig Karl, and Wilhelm Karl Grimm, *The German Legends of the Brothers Grimm.* Vol. 1. Ed. and transl. by Donald Ward. Philadelphia: Institute for the Study of Human Issues, 1981.

Hadfield, Miles, and John Hadfield, *The Twelve Days of Christmas.* Boston: Little, Brown and Company, 1961.*

Harrison, Shirley, *Who Is Father Christmas?* Newton Abbot, England: David & Charles, 1981.

Hastings, James, ed.:
Dictionary of the Bible. New York: Charles Scribner's Sons, 1909.
Encyclopaedia of Religion and Ethics. Vol. 3. New York: Charles Scribner's Sons, 1928.

Hawkes, Jacquetta, *Man and the Sun.* New York: Random House, 1962.

Heath, Edward, comp., *The Joy of Christmas: A Selection of Carols.* New York: Oxford University Press, 1978.

Henriksen, Vera, *Christmas in Norway: Past and Present.* Oslo: Tanum-Norli, 1981.

Hervey, Thomas K., *The Book of Christmas; Descriptive of the Customs, Ceremonies, Traditions, Superstitions, Fun, Feeling, and Festivities of the Christmas Season.* London: Frederick Warne & Co., 1888.

Hoffmann, E.T.A., *The Best Tales of Hoffmann.* Ed. by E. F. Bleiler. New York: Dover Publications, 1967.

Hole, Christina:
British Folk Customs. London: Hutchinson & Co., 1976.*
Christmas and Its Customs. New York: M. Barrows and Company, 1958.*

Holmberg, Uno, *Finno-Ugric, Siberian.* Vol. 4 of *The Mythology of All Races.* Ed. by John Arnott MacCulloch. New York: Cooper Square, 1964.

Hottes, Alfred Carl, *1001 Christmas Facts and Fancies.* New York: A. T. De La Mare Company, 1944.*

Hughes, David, *The Star of Bethlehem: An Astronomer's Confirmation.* New York: Walker and Company, 1979.

Ickis, Marguerite, *The Book of Christmas.* New York: Dodd, Mead & Company, 1960.

Jacobus de Voragine, *The Golden Legend of Jacobus de Voragine.* Transl. and adapted by Granger Ryan and Helmut Ripperger. New York: Arno Press, 1969.

Jones, E. Willis, *The Santa Claus Book.* New York: Walker and Company, 1976.

Jones, Gwyn, *Scandinavian Legends and Folk-tales.* London: Oxford University Press, 1956.

Krythe, Maymie R., *All about Christmas.* New York: Harper & Brothers, 1954.*

Lawson, John Cuthbert, *Modern Greek Folklore and Ancient Greek Religion: A Study in Survivals.* New Hyde Park, New York: University Books, 1964.

Leach, Maria, ed., *Funk & Wagnalls Standard Dictionary of Folklore, Mythology and Legend.* 2 vols. New York: Funk & Wagnalls, 1949.

Lindow, John, *Swedish Legends and Folktales.* Berkeley, California: University of California Press, 1978.

Littlewood, S. R., *The Story of Santa Claus.* London: Herbert & Daniel, 1912.*

McGinley, Phyllis, *A Wreath of Christmas Legends.* New York: The Macmillan Company, 1967.

McKnight, George H., *St. Nicholas: His Legend and His Role in the Christmas Celebration and Other Popular Customs.* Williamstown, Massachusetts: Corner House Publishers, 1974 (reprint of 1917 edition).

Manker, Ernst, *People of Eight Seasons: The Story of the Lapps.* New York: The Viking Press, 1964.

Maxym, Lucy, *Russian Lacquer, Legends and Fairy Tales.* Manhasset, New York: Siamese Imports, 1981.

Mid-Winter Festivals: Anthology of Stories, Traditions and Poems. Champaign, Illinois: Steven E. Clapp, 1984 (privately published).*

Miles, Clement A., *Christmas in Ritual and Tradition: Christian and Pagan*. London: T. Fisher Unwin, 1912.*

Muir, Frank, *Christmas Customs & Traditions*. New York: Taplinger Publishing Company, 1977.

Munch, Peter Andreas, *Norse Mythology: Legends of Gods and Heroes*. Transl. by Sigurd Bernhard Hustvedt. New York: AMS Press, 1970.

Newell, Venetia, *Discovering the Folklore of Birds and Beasts*. Tring, England: Shire Publications, 1971.

O'Shea, Denis, *The First Christmas*. Milwaukee, Wisconsin: The Bruce Publishing Company, 1952.

Pringle, Mary P., and Clara A. Urann, *Yule-tide in Many Lands*. Boston: Lothrop, Lee & Shepard Company, 1916.*

Rappoport, A. S., *Mediaeval Legends of Christ*. Norwood, Pennsylvania: Norwood Editions, 1977 (reprint of 1934 edition).

Sandys, William, *Christmas Carols, Ancient and Modern; Including the Most Popular in the West of England, and the Airs to Which They Are Sung*. Norwood, Pennsylvania: Norwood Editions, 1973 (reprint of 1833 edition).

Sansom, William, *A Book of Christ-*

mas. New York: McGraw-Hill Book Company, 1968.*

Sayre, Eleanor, ed., *A Christmas Book: Fifty Carols and Poems from the 14th to the 17th Centuries*. New York: Clarkson N. Potter, 1966.

Shekerjian, Haig, and Regina Shekerjian, comps., *A Book of Christmas Carols*. New York: Harper & Row, 1963.

Simon, Henry W., ed., *Christmas Songs and Carols*. Boston: Houghton Mifflin Company, 1973.

Simpson, Jacqueline, *Icelandic Folktales and Legends*. Berkeley, California: University of California Press, 1972.

Spicer, Dorothy Gladys, *46 Days of Christmas: A Cycle of Old World Songs, Legends and Customs*. New York: Coward-McCann, 1960.

Stevens, Patricia Bunning, *Merry Christmas! A History of the Holiday*. New York: Macmillan Publishing Co., 1979.

Swire, Otta F., *The Outer Hebrides and Their Legends*. Edinburgh, Scotland: Oliver & Boyd, 1966.

Taylor, Cyril, ed., *The Hawthorn Book of Christmas Carols*. New York: Hawthorn Books, 1957.

Then, John N., *Christmas Comes Again*. Milwaukee, Wisconsin: The Bruce Publishing Company, 1939.

Thonger, Richard, *A Calendar of Ger-*

man Customs. London: Oswald Wolff, 1966.

Tille, Alexander, *Yule and Christmas: Their Place in the Germanic Year*. London: David Nutt, 1899.

Toulson, Shirley, *The Winter Solstice*. London: Jill Norman & Hobhouse, 1981.*

Urlin, Ethel L., *Festivals, Holy Days, and Saints' Days: A Study in Origins and Survivals in Church Ceremonies & Secular Customs*. Ann Arbor, Michigan: Gryphon Books, 1971 (reprint).

Warren, Nathan Boughton, comp., *Christmas in the Olden Time: Its Customs and Their Origin*. Folcroft, Pennsylvania: Folcroft Library Editions, 1976 (reprint of 1859 edition).

Watts, Alan W., *Myth and Ritual in Christianity*. Boston: Beacon Press, 1970.*

Wernecke, Herbert H., *Christmas Customs around the World*. Philadelphia: The Westminster Press, no date.*

Wernecke, Herbert H., comp., *Carols, Customs and Costumes around the World*. Webster Groves, Missouri: The Old Orchard Book Shoppe, 1936.

Titles marked with an asterisk were especially helpful in the preparation of this volume.

Picture Credits

The sources for the illustrations in this book are shown below. When it is known, the name of the artist precedes the source of the picture.

Cover: Artwork by Michael Hague. 1, 3: Artwork by Michael Hague. 6: Artwork by Susan Gallagher. 7-135: Decorative borders by Alicia Austin. 9-15: Artwork by Susan Gallagher. 18-37: Artwork by Michael Hague. 38: Artwork by Troy Howell. 43: Artwork by Matt Mahurin. 44: Artwork by John Howe. 46, 47: Artwork by Matt Mahurin. 49: Artwork by John Howe. 50, 51: Artwork by Kinuko Y. Craft. 52: Artwork by John Howe. 54, 55: Artwork by Gary Kelley. 56-59: Artwork by Winslow Pels. 60: Artwork by John Howe. 62-77: Artwork by Roberto Innocenti. 78-84: Artwork by Troy Howell. 87: Artwork by Gary Kelley. 88, 89: Artwork by Troy Howell. 93-97: Artwork by Pauline Ellison. 98: Artwork by John Howe. 100, 101: Artwork by Winslow Pels. 102: Victor Vasnetsov, courtesy Tretyakov Gallery, photographed by M. Mesentsev, Moscow. 104-127: Artwork by Yvonne Gilbert. 128-133: Artwork by Susan Gallagher. 136, 137: Artwork by Yvonne Gilbert. 143, 144: Artwork by Michael Hague.

Time-Life Books Inc.
is a wholly owned subsidiary of

TIME INCORPORATED

FOUNDER: Henry R. Luce 1898-1967

Editor-in-Chief: Henry Anatole Grunwald
President: J. Richard Munro
Chairman of the Board: Ralph P. Davidson
Corporate Editor: Ray Cave
Group Vice President, Books: Reginald K. Brack Jr.
Vice President, Books: George Artandi

TIME-LIFE BOOKS INC.

EDITOR: George Constable
Director of Design: Louis Klein
Editorial General Manager: Neal Goff
Director of Editorial Resources: Phyllis K. Wise
Acting Text Director: Ellen Phillips
Editorial Board: Russell B. Adams Jr., Dale M.
Brown, Roberta Conlan, Thomas H. Flaherty
Jr., Donia Ann Steele, Rosalind Stubenberg,
Kit van Tulleken, Henry Woodhead
Director of Photography and Research: John
Conrad Weiser

PRESIDENT: Reginald K. Brack Jr.
Executive Vice Presidents: John M. Fahey Jr.,
Christopher T. Linen
Senior Vice President: James L. Mercer
Vice Presidents: Stephen L. Bair, Edward Brash,
Ralph J. Cuomo, Juanita T. James, Hallett
Johnson III, Robert H. Smith, Paul R.
Stewart, Leopoldo Toralballa
Director of Production Services: Robert J.
Passantino

THE ENCHANTED WORLD

SERIES DIRECTOR: Ellen Phillips
Deputy Editor: Robin Richman
Designer: Dale Pollekoff
Series Administrator: Jane Edwin

Editorial Staff for *The Book of Christmas*
Researcher: Charlotte Marine Fullerton
Assistant Designer: Lorraine D. Rivard
Copy Coordinators: Barbara Fairchild
Quarmby, Robert M. S. Somerville
Picture Coordinator: Bradley Hower
Editorial Assistant: Constance B. Strawbridge

Editorial Operations
Copy Chief: Diane Ullius
Editorial Operations: Caroline A.
Boubin (manager)
Production: Celia Beattie
Quality Control: James J. Cox (director)
Library: Louise D. Forstall

Correspondents: Elisabeth Kraemer-Singh
(Bonn); Dorothy Bacon (London); Maria
Vincenza Aloisi, Josephine du Brusle (Paris);
Ann Natanson (Rome). Valuable assistance
was also provided by: Mirka Gondicas (Athens); Angelika Lemmer (Bonn); Gevene
Hertz (Copenhagen); Milly Trowbridge
(London); Trini Bandrés (Madrid); Felix Rosenthal (Moscow); Dag Christensen (Oslo);
Thorstein Tthorarenson (Reykjavik); Mary
Johnson (Stockholm).

The Author

Brendan Lehane was born in London
of Irish parents. A graduate of
Cambridge University, he was a magazine journalist before launching a career as an author. His books include
The Companion Guide to Ireland, *The Complete Flea*, *The Quest of Three Abbots* and
The Power of Plants. For Time-Life Books
he has written *Dublin* in The Great
Cities series and *The Northwest Passage* in
The Seafarers series, as well as *Wizards
and Witches* and *Legends of Valor* in The
Enchanted World series.

Chief Series Consultant

Tristram Potter Coffin, Professor of
English at the University of Pennsylvania, is a leading authority on folklore.
He is the author or editor of numerous
books and more than one hundred articles. His best-known works are *The British Traditional Ballad in North America*, *The
Old Ball Game*, *The Book of Christmas Folklore* and *The Female Hero*.

This volume is one of a series that is based
on myths, legends and folk tales.

Other Publications:

HEALTHY HOME COOKING
UNDERSTANDING COMPUTERS
YOUR HOME
THE KODAK LIBRARY OF CREATIVE PHOTOGRAPHY
GREAT MEALS IN MINUTES
THE CIVIL WAR
PLANET EARTH
COLLECTOR'S LIBRARY OF THE CIVIL WAR
THE EPIC OF FLIGHT
THE GOOD COOK
WORLD WAR II
HOME REPAIR AND IMPROVEMENT
THE OLD WEST

For information on and a full description
of any of the Time-Life Books series listed
above, please write:
Reader Information
Time-Life Books
541 North Fairbanks Court
Chicago, Illinois 60611

© 1986 Time-Life Books Inc. All rights reserved. No part of this book may be reproduced in any form or by any electronic or
mechanical means, including information
storage and retrieval devices or systems,
without prior written permission from the
publisher, except that brief passages may be
quoted for reviews.
First printing. Printed in U.S.A.
Published simultaneously in Canada.
School and library distribution by Silver
Burdett Company, Morristown, New Jersey
07960.

TIME-LIFE is a trademark of Time
Incorporated U.S.A.

Library of Congress Cataloguing
in Publication Data
Lehane, Brendan.
     The book of Christmas.
     (The Enchanted world)
     Bibliography: p.
     1. Christmas. I. Time-Life Books.
II. Title.   III. Series.
GT4985.L44 1986   394.2'68282   86-11220
ISBN 0-8094-5261-8
ISBN 0-8094-5262-6 (lib. bdg.)

Time-Life Books Inc. offers a wide range of
fine recordings, including a *Big Bands* series.
For subscription information, call 1-800-621-
7026 or write TIME-LIFE MUSIC, Time &
Life Building, Chicago, Illinois 60611.

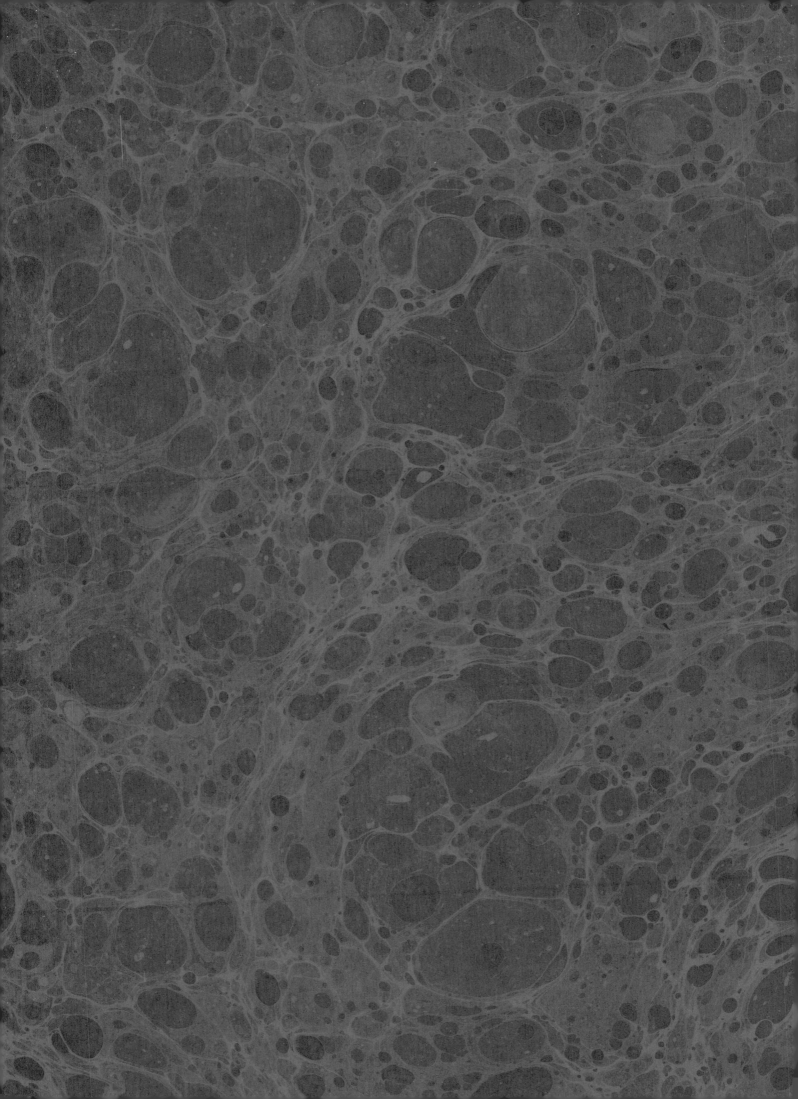